The
Imitation of Christ

THE FOLLOWING OF CHRIST—"Anyone who wishes to follow Me must deny self, take up the cross, and follow Me" (Mk 8:34).

THE
IMITATION OF CHRIST

IN FOUR BOOKS
BY
THOMAS A KEMPIS

Newly Edited by
CLARE L. FITZPATRICK

NEW ILLUSTRATED EDITION

CATHOLIC BOOK PUBLISHING CORP.
NEW YORK

NIHIL OBSTAT: Daniel V. Flynn, J.C.D.
Censor Librorum

IMPRIMATUR: ✠ Joseph T. O'Keefe, D.D.
Vicar General, Archbishop of New York

To my dear friend,
FATHER WALTER VAN DE PUTTE, C.S.SP.,
without whose help and encouragement
this work would never have been undertaken.

(T-320)

Printed in China

3 4 5 6 7 8 9 10 11 12 13 14 15

Foreword

OUR Lord's words *"Anyone who wishes to follow Me must deny self, take up the cross daily and follow Me"* (Lk 9:23) were spoken for people of all times and localities. They are equally applicable to the young, to the middle aged and to the elderly. They are a challenge to modern people—so surrounded by the comforts and conveniences of modern inventions—who take all these things for granted and, becoming immersed in the material, often forget their eternal destiny.

How often do we say, and hear others say: "Oh, if only I could have a little peace!" Perhaps our greatest hindrance to this peace we all desire so much is the constant urge to lift the veil and see what tomorrow will bring. We are surrounded by this attitude; our weather forecasts are all occupied with what is coming next. So we let today's moments slip by us almost unheeded.

One of the lessons our Lord teaches His followers is that we are not promised the whole of today: *The Son of Man will come at an hour when you do not expect Him* (Mt 24:44). Therefore, it is well for us to live our lives each day fully. You will say perhaps that your life is full, that you are on the go every minute. But we forget that we are made up of body and soul and all this hyperactivity leaves no time for the soul to breathe.

As you thoughtfully and prayerfully read this book, turn the pages slowly and allow the wisdom contained in them to penetrate your inner self. If you will do this, you will find a great peace—even amid the turmoil around you and the trials that necessarily come into every life. The Holy Spirit will bring you His peace and His joy that you will never find in any of the thing which the world promises you, but which promises are never kept.

It is the fervent hope of the publisher of this new edition of THE IMITATION OF CHRIST that this treasured little book will become a daily reminder of and a spur to follow the life of Christ to which all are called.

CONTENTS

BOOK 1: USEFUL ADMONITIONS FOR THE SPIRITUAL LIFE

BOOK 4: ON THE BLESSED SACRAMENT AND DEVOUT EXHORTATIONS FOR HOLY COMMUNION

JESUS OPENS OUR EYES TO FOLLOW HIM—"Jesus said to [the blind man], 'Receive your sight. Your faith has made you well.' Immediately, he received his sight and followed Jesus" (Lk 18:42f).

BOOK 1

USEFUL ADMONITIONS FOR THE SPIRITUAL LIFE

CHAPTER 1

On Following Christ Our Model

NO ONE *who follows Me will ever walk in darkness* (Jn 8:12). These words of our Lord counsel all to walk in His footsteps. If you want to see clearly and avoid blindness of heart, it is His virtues you must imitate. Make it your aim to meditate on the life of Jesus Christ.

2. Christ's teaching surpasses that of all the Saints. But to find this spiritual nourishment you must seek to have the Spirit of Christ. It is because we lack this Spirit that so often we listen to the Gospel without really hearing it. Those who fully understand Christ's words must labor to make their lives conform to His.

3. To be learned and able to discuss the Trinity will get you nowhere if you do not have humility, and therefore displease the Holy Trinity. Lofty words neither save you nor make you a Saint;

only a virtuous life makes you dear to God. It is better to experience contrition than to be able to define it.

To be well versed in Scripture and all the sayings of philosophers will not profit you if you are without God's love and His grace. *All things are vanity* (Eccl 1:2). Nothing matters except to love God and to serve Him only. The height of wisdom is to set your goal on heaven by despising the world.

4. How foolish it is to seek and to put your trust in riches that will pass. How foolish to go after worldly honors and to set yourself above others. How foolish to follow the impulses of the flesh, or to covet those things which so soon will cost you a heavy penalty.

How foolish to wish for a long life, but not care whether it is a good life; to be concerned only with the present, with never a thought of eternity and the endless joy that awaits you.

5. Often think of the proverb: *"The eye is not satisfied with seeing, nor is the ear filled with hearing"* (Eccl 1:8). Be determined to detach your heart from the love of visible things, allowing it to center on those unseen.

CHAPTER 2

On Having a Humble Opinion of Oneself

KNOWLEDGE is a natural desire in all people. But knowledge for its own sake is useless unless you fear God. An unlearned peasant, whose contentment is the service of God, is far better than the learned and the clever, whose pride in their knowledge leads them to neglect their souls while fixing their attention on the stars.

True self-knowledge makes you aware of your own worthlessness and you will take no pleasure in the praises of others. If your knowledge encompasses the universe and the love of God is not in you, what good will it do you in God's sight? He will judge you according to your actions.

2. An overweening desire for knowledge brings many distractions and much delusion. Many like to be considered learned and to be praised for their wisdom; how much knowledge there is which adds nothing to the good of the soul! To spend yourself on worldly pursuits which do nothing to further your eternal salvation is unwise.

It is useless to spend much time in talking; only a holy life and a good conscience will ease your mind and satisfy your soul, enabling you to face God with confidence.

3. Remember, the more you know, the more severely you will be judged. So do not be proud of any skill or knowledge you may have, for such is an awesome responsibility. No matter how much you know, realize how much there is that you do not know. Do not be afraid to acknowledge your own ignorance.

Why have an exalted opinion of yourself when you know there are many, even in your own field, whose knowledge surpasses yours? If you want to learn anything worthwhile, seek rather to be unknown and to be thought of as nothing.

4. Nothing is so beneficial as a true knowledge of ourselves, which produces a wholesome self-contempt. Always think kindly of others, while holding yourself as nothing; this is true wisdom and leads to perfection. If you see another commit a grievous sin, or whose faults are flagrant, do not regard yourself as better, for you do not know what you would do if similarly tempted. You are in good disposition now, but you do not know how long you will persevere in it. Always keep in mind that all are frail, but none so frail as yourself.

CHAPTER 3

On the Teaching of Truth

PERSONS who are taught by truth and not by symbols or deceitful words are really blessed and happy, for they learn truth in itself. Our own opinions and lack of knowledge often lead us astray, because we do not know the truth as it is.

What good will it do us to learn many things, the knowledge of which will not help us on judgment day, nor hurt us if we do not know them? It is foolish not to learn those things which are necessary for us and to waste our time on those that merely satisfy our curiosity and hurt us in the end. For if we do so, we have eyes but cannot see.

2. What need have we to be concerned with unessentials? He to whom the Eternal Word (Who is Jesus) speaks is freed of useless opinions. From the Word all things proceed and all creation cries out that He is God—the same Who is

the Beginning Who speaks to us. No one can understand the truth nor make right judgments without Him. Only those to whom all things are One, who draw all things to One and who see all things in One, may be strong in heart and rest peacefully in God.

O my God, You are Truth; unite me to Yourself in perfect love. I am so weary of all I read and hear and see, for only in You is all that I will or can desire. Let all the learned be silent in Your presence and let all creatures be still and do You, Lord, alone speak to my soul.

3. The more we are united within ourselves and are joined to You in the simplicity of our hearts, the more effortlessly we understand the deep things, for the light of understanding comes to us from above. A pure, simple and stable heart is not bogged down by a multitude of tasks because it does all for the honor of God, and since it is not self-seeking, it is not eager to follow its own will.

An unmortified spirit is your greatest hindrance. Good and devout people first plan inwardly the works they are to do outwardly; in this way they are not led to evil inclinations, but bend their wills to the rule of right reason. Who has a greater struggle than those who labor to overcome themselves? This should be our daily labor: self-conquest, so as to make steady progress in the spiritual life.

4. There is no absolute perfection in this life, for there is always some imperfection attached to

it; likewise there is no knowledge in this world that is not mixed with some ignorance. Therefore, a humble self-knowledge is a surer way to God than a search after deep learning.

It is not wrong to pursue learning, for since it comes from God it is good as far as it goes; but it is far better to have a clean conscience and lead a virtuous life. Because some prefer to be learned than to be virtuous, they make many mistakes and produce little or no fruit.

If only people would use as much energy in avoiding sin and cultivating virtues as they do in disputing questions, there would not be so much evil in the world, nor bad example given, nor would there be so much laxity in religion!

On the day of judgment we will not be asked what we have read, but what we have done; neither will we be asked how well we have spoken, but how devoutly we have lived. Where are all the Doctors and learned people who were famous in their day? They are now supplanted by others. In their lifetime they enjoyed fame, but now they are scarcely remembered.

5. How quickly the glory of this world passes, with its deceptive pleasures! If only their life had been on a par with their learning, then all their study and reading would have been to a good end. Many there are who care little for a good life in the service of God, because they give themselves up to useless pursuits. They prefer to be great in this world than to be humble, and therefore their illusions go up in smoke.

Those who abound in charity are truly great; and those are also great who are little in their own estimation and regard all worldly honors as nothing. How wise are those who look upon worldly pleasures as dung in order to gain Christ. They are truly learned who forsake their own will to follow the will of God.

CHAPTER 4

On Being Prudent in What We Accept and Do

IT IS not good to be taken in by every word or impulse that comes our way, but consider the thing prudently and thoughtfully in order not to offend God. Because we are frail we are always ready to believe the worst of people. Those who seek perfection realize that human nature is weak and prone to spread the evil word.

2. It is wise, therefore, to act slowly, not to trust entirely our own opinions, or to accept every tale and quickly pass it along to the next one. Seek advice from a wise person of good conscience and be instructed by that person rather than follow your own way. A good life will make you wise in the ways of God and will broaden your experience. If you are humble and submissive to God's will, you will have peace in all you do.

CHAPTER 5

On the Reading of Holy Scripture

IT IS truth that must be sought in Holy Scripture, not beauty of expression. It should be

THE SPIRIT GUIDES US IN READING SCRIPTURE—"When [the Paraclete] the Spirit of truth comes, He will guide you into all the truth" (Jn 16:13).

read with the same spirit in which it was written. We must seek the good of our soul rather than literary style, and just as gladly read simple and devout books as those of deep and subtle learning.

Be concerned only with the pure truth in what you read and not with the greatness or lack of learning of the author. Think more of what is said than of the one who said it.

2. Humans soon pass away; *the truth of the Lord remains forever* (Ps 117:2). Through the Scripture God speaks to us in many ways, regardless of those He uses as instruments. Too often we are led by curiosity to read Holy Scripture and want to understand and argue passages we should simply pass over.

If you wish to profit by the reading of Scripture, then do so with humility, simplicity and faith and never try to acquire a reputation for being a scholar. Inquire, and then listen meekly to what the Saints tell you. Do not be critical of the sayings of the ancient Fathers, for they were not written without reason.

CHAPTER 6

Concerning Inordinate Affections

WHEN people desire anything to an excessive degree, they immediately lose their peace of soul. The proud and avaricious are always perturbed; while the humble and the poor in spirit live in peace and contentment. Those who are not mortified are easily overcome by small temptations.

It is difficult for people to withdraw themselves from worldly desires when their spirits are still weak and inclined to the things of sense. While in this state their hearts are heavy when they try to detach themselves and they are quickly angered by those who oppose them.

2. If they give in to themselves, then they suffer remorse of conscience because they have yielded to temptation and do not find the peace of mind they desired. We find our peace only by resisting our passions, not by giving in to them.

Peace is in the heart of the devout and fervent, not in those who are carnal and give themselves to outward things.

CHAPTER 7

On False Confidence and Arrogance

IT IS foolish to put your trust in humans—or in any creature for that matter. Why should you mind serving others or being poor in the eyes of the world, as long as you do it for the love of Jesus Christ? Put all your confidence in God, but do not trust yourself.

Do what you can to please Him and He will reward you well for your good will. Do not trust your own cleverness nor that of any person; rather, put your trust in the grace of God, Who gives aid to the humble but humiliates the presumptuous.

2. Do not boast of riches if you have them, or of your important friends; but glory in God only, from Whom all good things come and Who, being the highest good, desires to give us Him-

self. Do not boast of beauty of body, which is soon disfigured by illness or age. Do not be proud of any talents or skills you possess, for in this way you displease God from Whom you have received them.

3. Do not consider yourself better than others, for you may be worse in God's sight. Do not be proud of your good works, for often what pleases us displeases God, Whose judgments differ from the judgment of humans. Whatever goodness or virtue is in you, believe that your neighbor has better qualities; in this way you will preserve humility.

It will not hurt you to consider yourself worse than others, even if this is not really so; but it will hurt greatly if you prefer yourself above another, although that person might be a great sinner. A humble person is a peaceful person; but the hearts of the proud are full of envy and resentment.

CHAPTER 8

On Avoiding Too Much Familiarity

DO NOT open your heart to everyone, but only to one who is wise, God-fearing, and who can keep your confidence. Spend little time in the company of young people or with the inexperienced; do not flatter the rich, or seek to be in the presence of the great without good reason.

Rather associate yourself with those who are humble and have simplicity, who are devout and self-disciplined, talking with them about those things that will edify and strengthen the soul. Do not be familiar with the opposite sex, but commend to God those who are good. Desire to be on intimate terms with God and His Angels, but shun the acquaintance of people as much as you can.

2. Have charity for all; but familiarity is unwise. Sometimes it happens that we know someone only by fame, but when we meet that person we are often disappointed. And sometimes we think we please others by our presence, when in reality they come to dislike us because of the faults they see in us.

CHAPTER 9

On Being Obedient and Submissive

TO BE obedient, to live under a superior—not seeking our own way—is great virtue. It is safer to obey orders than to give them. Many obey more out of necessity than for charity's sake. These find it burdensome and complain easily; but they will never have liberty of spirit until they submit wholly to authority for the love of God.

Go where you will, but you will never find rest except in humble obedience to the rule of your superior. Many are deceived by thinking that a change of location will solve their difficulties.

2. In reality, all of us are inclined to do our own will and agree more readily with those who hold with our views. But if we want to have the presence of God among us, then we must be willing to give up our own way in order to live in love

and harmony with others. Surely there are no persons so wise that they know everything.

Therefore, listen to the opinions of others and do not trust too much in your own point of view. Perhaps you are right, but by setting aside your own will and following another out of love for God, you will profit by it.

3. I have often heard it said that it is surer to take advice than to give it! It is good to listen to every person's advice; but when it is sound, to disagree is sheer stubbornness.

CHAPTER 10

On Avoiding Superfluous Words

FLEE as much as possible the company of worldly people. For discussing worldly matters, no matter how good the intention, is a great obstacle to the spiritual life. If we are not careful, we can be easily deceived and attracted by the vanity of the world. Often I regret the things I have said and wished that I had not spent so much time in worldly company.

We think that by getting together with others we will be a comfort to one another and find relaxation by discussing the things that burden us; but the end result of all this gossip about things we like or dislike only leaves us with a guilty conscience.

2. But the sad part of it is that all we say and do is for nothing; for the comfort we receive from others hinders us from receiving the comfort that comes from God. It is better to watch and pray so

that we do not waste time in idleness. If you have leave to speak and it is expedient, then speak of God and of those things which will edify.

A bad use or neglect of our spiritual progress makes us careless of what we say. However, devout conversation on spiritual matters is beneficial to the soul, especially when people who are congenial in mind and spirit are drawn together in God.

CHAPTER 11

On How to Acquire Peace and on the Desire to Improve

WE WOULD indeed have peace if we would attend to our affairs. How can you remain in peace when you deliberately interfere in other people's business and seek worldly occupation with seldom a thought to interior recollection? The humble and the single-hearted are truly blessed and will have abundant peace.

2. The reason why the Saints were so perfectly recollected is that they always sought to abstain from worldly desires, leaving themselves free to give their whole heart to God. But we are absorbed in our own passions and too concerned with passing things. We seldom overcome even one single fault; we are slow to make progress and therefore remain cold and indifferent.

3. If we would die to self-love, soon we would enjoy spiritual things and then we would experience heavenly contemplation. As it is, we do not force ourselves to overcome our passions and disorderly desires and to follow the path of the

Saints and this is our greatest obstacle to contemplation. As soon as any little difficulty comes our way, we are easily cast down and turn to human consolation.

4. If only we would exert ourselves and take a firm stand in this battle, we would see how God comes to our aid, for He is always ready to help those who put their trust in Him. He even provides occasions for us to do battle so that we will overcome and be victorious.

If our religion consists only in outward observances, our piety will soon come to an end. We had better lay our axe to the root, that being purged from our passions, we may possess our soul in peace.

5. If we would overcome one fault a year we would soon be perfect! But often we find that we were better and purer when we first turned to God than after years supposedly spent in His service. Actually, our fervor and desire for virtue should increase every day as we grow older.

But now it is considered wonderful if we still hold onto a spark of our first fervor. It is far easier to break evil habits at the outset, for then acts of virtue are done more easily and with a happy heart.

6. It is not easy to break bad habits and harder still to give up your own will. But if you do not overcome the little things, how do you expect to overcome the greater? Therefore, resist your evil inclinations at the start and break off bad habits,

or little by little they will lead you into greater difficulties.

If only you would think of the great interior peace you would have and how happy you would make others by doing good, you would be more eager to grow in virtue!

CHAPTER 12

On the Advantage of Not Having Everything Our Own Way

IT IS good that everything is not always to our liking; for adversity makes people look into their hearts in order to realize that they are exiles and must not put their hopes in any worldly thing.

It is good for us to run into opposition and to have others think badly of us, even when our intentions are good. For these things help us to be humble and rid us of pride. Then we seek God more earnestly, Who alone knows our inmost self, when outwardly we are ignored and discredited by others.

2. Therefore, people should rely so entirely on God that they have no need to look for human consolations when adversity comes. When people of good disposition are afflicted or tempted or distracted by evil thoughts, then they understand the need they have of God and that without Him they can do nothing.

Then too they grieve, while they sigh and pray because of the miseries they endure. They grow weary of this life and long for death in order to be with Christ, their Lord. It will also be clear to them that there is neither perfect peace nor security in this world.

CHAPTER 13

On Resisting Temptation

WE WILL never be free of trials and temptations as long as our earthly life lasts. For Job has said: *"Is not the life of human beings on earth a drudgery?"* (Job 7:1). Therefore, we should always be on our guard against temptations, always praying that our enemy, the devil, *who never sleeps but constantly looks for someone to devour* (1 Pet 5:8), will not catch us off guard.

No one in this world is so perfect or holy as not to have temptations sometimes. We can never be entirely free of them.

2. Sometimes these temptations can be very severe and troublesome, but if we resist them, they will be very useful to us; for by experiencing them we are humbled, cleansed and instructed. All the Saints endured tribulations and temptations and profited by them, while those who did not resist and overcome them fell away and were lost.

There is no place so holy or so remote where you will not meet with temptation, nor is there anyone completely free from it in this life; for in our body we bear the wounds of sin—the weakness of our human nature in which we were born.

3. As soon as one temptation or trial goes, another comes. We will always have something to

suffer because we have lost our original state of happiness.

Many try to fly away from temptations only to fall more deeply into them; for you cannot win a battle by mere flight. It is only by patience and humility that you will be strengthened against the enemy.

4. Those who only shun them outwardly and do not pull them out by the roots will make no progress; for temptations will soon return to harass them and they will be in a worse state. It is only gradually—with patience and endurance and with God's grace—that you will overcome temptations sooner than by your own efforts and anxieties.

When you are tempted seek the advice of a wise counselor, and do not yourself be harsh with persons who are tempted; rather be happy to console them as you would wish to be consoled.

5. The beginning of all evil temptations is inconstancy of mind and insufficient trust in God. Just as a ship without a rudder is tossed about with every storm, so those who are negligent and abandon their good resolutions are tempted in diverse ways. Gold is tried by fire and the upright person by temptation. Often we do not know what we can do until temptation shows us what we are.

In the early stages of temptation it is necessary to be watchful, for it is easier to overcome the enemy if he is not allowed to enter into your mind, but is resisted and shut out as soon as he knocks. As someone has said: "Resist the beginning; the cure applied afterward is too late."

This is how temptation is: first we have a thought, followed by strong imaginings, then the pleasure and evil emotions, and finally consent. This is how the enemy gains full admittance, because he was not resisted at the outset. The slower we are to resist, the weaker we daily become and the stronger the enemy is against us.

6. Temptations differ with different people: some are greatly tempted in the first stages of turning to God; some have it in their later days; while still others have it all their lives, and there are also those who are only lightly tempted. But it is all part of God's plan for us, Whose wisdom and justice knows each person's state and orders all things rightly for the salvation of His elect.

7. We should not be discouraged when tempted, but turn in fervent prayer to God, Who, in His infinite goodness and compassion, will help us in all our needs. St. Paul has said that *"together with the trial He will also provide a way out and the strength to bear it"* (1 Cor 10:13).

Let us humbly submit ourselves to God in all trials and temptations, for *it is the humble and submissive that He will save and exalt* (Ps 34:19).

8. Through temptations and trials our spiritual progress is tested. If we are fervent and devout and unaware of any difficulties, it is no credit to us; but if we endure patiently in the time of temptation or adversity, then our spiritual advancement is apparent.

Some people are kept from grave temptations and yet every day they fall into the same petty faults. God in His merciful goodness permits this to keep them humble, so that they will not trust in themselves, seeing how easily they are daily overcome.

CHAPTER 14

On Avoiding Hasty Judgments

WATCH over yourself and take care not to judge the actions of other people. We gain nothing by criticizing others, but often are mistaken and thereby offend God. But to judge yourself and your own actions is always profitable.

We often judge a thing according to our preference and therefore our judgment is emotional rather than objective. This stubbornness in our own opinions would not dominate our judgments if our hearts were set on God.

2. But there is often in us some inward tendency or some outward attraction which carries us along with it. Many are secretly self-seeking and therefore do their own will and not the will of God, though sometimes they are unaware of it.

As long as things go their way, they appear to be at peace, but if they meet opposition, they become impatient and depressed. Often through diversities of opinions dissension springs up between friends and neighbors and even among religious and devout persons.

3. An old habit is not easily overcome, and people are reluctant to be led beyond their own views. If you cling more to your own reason or

will rather than to humble obedience of Jesus Christ, you will only with difficulty become an enlightened person. For it is the will of God that we be perfectly subject to Him, rising above our own reason and will by an ardent love.

CHAPTER 15

On Works Done from the Motive of Charity

NEVER is evil to be done for any worldly gain nor for love of any human being. But there are times when a good deed may be deferred for the benefit of one who is in need, or it can be changed to a better deed. In that way the good planned is not undone, but rather is transformed into something better.

Without charity the outward deed is worthless; but whatever is done out of charity, no matter how small and insignificant, is profitable in the eyes of God, Who looks not so much at what we do, as to the love with which we do it.

2. Those who love God much do much, and those do a deed well who perform it for the common good and not to please themselves. Often what appears to be charity is really done for carnal motives—self-love, the hope of a reward or some personal advantage seldom being absent.

3. True charity is not self-seeking, but goes all the way for the honor and glory of God. Those who are charitable envy no one, nor do they seek their own pleasure, but desire above all things to find their joy in God.

How well they know that no good begins in humans and so they refer all to God, from Whom all things come and in Whom all the Saints find their eternal blessedness. If they had only a spark of real charity, they would know in their souls that all earthly things are vain.

CHAPTER 16

On Bearing with the Defects of Others

THERE will always be defects in ourselves or others which we cannot correct. These we must simply tolerate until God in His goodness sees fit to change things. After all, this may be the best possible way to prove our patience, without which our good qualities are not worth much.

Nevertheless, you must pray earnestly that God in His mercy will help you to bear these impediments with patience.

2. If once or twice you have warned someone and that person does not comply, do not contend further with such a one, but leave all in the hands of God, that His will be done and that He be glorified in all His servants, for He knows well how to turn evil into good.

Learn how to be patient in enduring the faults of others, remembering that you yourself have many which others have to put up with. If you cannot make yourself be what you would like, how can you expect another to be as you would like? We wish to see perfection in others, but do not correct our own faults.

JESUS CALLS FOR RECONCILIATION BEFORE SACRIFICE— "Therefore, when offering your gift at the altar, if you should remember that you have treated your brother badly, leave your gift there at the altar and immediately go to be reconciled with your brother" (Mt 5:23f).

3. We want to have others strictly reprimanded for their offenses, but we will not be reprimanded ourselves. We are inclined to think the other person has too much liberty, but we ourselves will not put up with any restraint. There must be rules for everyone else, but we must be given free rein. It is seldom that we consider our neighbor equally with ourselves.

If everyone was perfect, what would we have to endure for the love of God?

4. God wills us to learn to bear one another's burdens. No one is without faults, no one without a cross, no one self-sufficient and no one wise enough all alone. Therefore, we must support, comfort and assist one another, instructing and admonishing one another in all charity.

Adversity is the best test of virtue. The occasions of sin do not weaken anyone; on the contrary, they show that person's true worth.

CHAPTER 17

On the Religious Life

IF YOU want to get along with others, it is necessary to curb your own will in many things. It is not easy to live in a monastery or a congregation, to remain there without complaint or reproof and to persevere in your vocation.

If you wish to remain steadfast in grace and to grow in virtue, consider yourself an exile and a pilgrim in this world. You must rejoice to be considered a fool and a contemptuous person for the love of God.

2. Receiving the habit and the tonsure is but little help; it is the reforming of your life and the dying to self-love that makes the true religious. If you seek anything in religious life other than God and the good of your soul, you will find nothing but trouble and grief and you will not persevere there in peace unless you strive to be the least and be subject to all.

3. It is good, therefore, often to remember that you entered religious life to serve and not to be served, and that you are called to suffer and to work, not to waste your time in idleness and gossip. In religious life you are meant to be tried as gold in a furnace and you will not last long unless with all your heart you are ready to humble yourself for the love of God.

CHAPTER 18

On the Examples Given by the Holy Fathers

LOOK at the shining examples of our ancient Fathers and the Saints, in whom true perfection and religion flourished and then you will see how little we do by comparison. How can we even compare our life with theirs!

These friends of Christ served Him amid all sorts of tribulations: hunger and thirst, heat and cold, labor and weariness, in vigils and fasts, holy meditations and prayers and in persecutions and insults.

2. Consider the many and grievous trials endured by the Apostles, Martyrs, Confessors, Virgins, and indeed all the Saints who followed in

the footsteps of our Lord! In order to possess everlasting life they rejected honors and all the pleasures of this life.

How strict and mortified was the life our Fathers led in the wilderness! How many grievous temptations they endured and violent assaults of the devil! How fervently they prayed daily to God, imposing rigid fasts on themselves! What ardent zeal to advance in the spiritual life! What relentless war they waged against all sin and with what pure and wholehearted intention did they aspire toward God!

3. They worked by day and they prayed by night. Their time was always profitably spent, for even in their physical labors they turned their minds to God and considered the time in His service all too short. Often they forgot the need for food, so consoling were their contemplations.

They abandoned riches, honors, friends and families; they wanted nothing of this world, scarcely even taking what was necessary for the body. Outwardly they were in need, but inwardly they were filled with grace and spiritual consolation.

4. They were strangers to the world, but to God they were dear and intimate friends. In the world's eyes and in their own they were despised as nothing; but in the eyes of God and His Saints they were beloved and precious indeed. True humility, simple obedience, charity, patience— in fact all the virtues shone forth in them.

This is why they grew spiritually every day, gaining great grace from God. They were given as an example to all who desire to be holy; how much more, therefore, should they inspire us to advance spiritually than the number of the lukewarm influence us to grow lax.

5. How fervent were the religious when their institutions were founded! What devotion in prayer, what zeal for virtue and what strict discipline was maintained! Reverence and obedience under the rule of the Superior prospered!

The history of their deeds bears witness to their holiness and perfection by which they were able to subdue the world and trample it beneath their feet. Nowadays, those who can keep the rule and maintain patience in what they have undertaken are thought the world of.

6. How sad it is that through our own negligence and wasting of time we have fallen so quickly from our first fervor, and are even tired of life itself! God grant that the desire to advance in virtue be not dormant in you, who so often have had the examples of the Saints before you!

CHAPTER 19

On the Exercises of a Good Religious

THE life of a good religious should be distinguished by virtue, being inwardly as one appears outwardly, for He Who sees the heart is God, Whom we should always reverence. We should walk in His Presence as pure as the Angels.

Every day renew your dedication to God, arousing fervent devotion in your heart as if it were the first day of your turning back to God. Pray to Him, saying: "Help me, Lord Jesus, to persevere in my good resolutions and in Your holy service till death. Help me to begin this day well, for up to now I have done nothing."

2. As our intention is, so will our progress be, and we have need of great diligence if we want to advance. For if those whose purpose is to do good often fall short of it, what shall the person do who seldom, if ever, makes such a resolution?

Let us then make up our minds to do the best we can; even so our good intention may be hindered in various ways, such as the omission of a good exercise for a slight reason. It is seldom that such willful omission can be recovered without spiritual loss.

The resolution of devout persons depends more on the grace of God than on their own wisdom. For human beings propose, but God disposes, *nor is the course of their life as they would have it* (Jer 10:23).

3. If for the sake of charity a pious practice is omitted, it may be recovered later; but if omitted through laziness or our own negligence, it is not a small fault and will prove harmful. Although we try our best, some failures will be unavoidable.

Nevertheless, we must have a resolve about something definite, particularly concerning those things which are our greatest hindrances. We should carefully search and put in order both our interior and exterior, for both are necessary to our spiritual progress.

4. If you cannot recollect yourself all the time, you should do so at intervals; for instance, in the morning you should make your resolution for the day, and then in the evening check up on yourself to see what your conduct has been during the day—how you have kept your resolution, what have been your thoughts, words and actions. For in any of these ways you may have offended God and your neighbor more often than you think.

Arm yourself with humility and charity so as to ward off the attacks of the devil. Refrain from gluttony and it will be easier for you to restrain carnal desires. Never be idle: read, write, meditate, pray, or work for the good of the community. As for bodily mortifications, practice these with discretion; for what is profitable for one may harm another.

5. Personal penitential practices are best done in private and not openly for others to see. Do not be more inclined to the devotions of your own choosing than to those that are of religious obligation. When you have faithfully fulfilled your obligation, then if there is time left, you may perform those devotions according to your inspiration.

The same pious practices are not practical for all; for one suits one person, while another suits someone else. Different exercises are required for different times, some being more applicable for holy days, others for ordinary days. Also, we need one kind in time of temptation and another in time of peace and quiet; one when we have devotion, another when devotion is absent.

6. As the principal feasts occur we must renew our pious practices according to the spirit of the feast, fervently asking the Saints to help us. As the liturgical year unfolds, we should make our resolutions as if we were then to leave this world for the everlasting feast in heaven.

In this way, we ought to prepare ourselves at holy seasons, living more devoutly and performing our duties more exactly as if we were soon to go before God to receive the reward of our labors.

7. But if it be delayed, we can be sure that we were neither ready nor prepared for that glory, which will be revealed to us in God's time. Let us then prepare ourselves better for the appointed time.

In St. Luke's Gospel we read: *"Blessed is that servant if his Master finds him [watching] when He arrives home. Truly I tell you, He will put him in charge of all His property"* (Lk 12:43, 44).

CHAPTER 20

On the Love of Solitude and Silence

SEEK a convenient time to search your own conscience, meditating on the benefits of God. Restrain curiosity; read only those things that will move you to contrition rather than give you distraction.

If you will withdraw from unnecessary talk and useless running about and listening to the latest gossip, you will find the time to occupy yourself in devout mediation. The greatest Saints avoided the company of worldly people as much as possible, for they preferred to be alone with God.

2. One person has said: “As often as I have been among others, I have returned less a man.” We know this from experience when we talk too long. It is easier to remain silent than not to say too much when we speak.

It is also easier to stay home alone than to watch what you say when you go out so as not to offend. Therefore, those who intend to lead the interior life and to have the grace of devotion must, with our Lord, go away from the crowd. Unless you like solitude, it is not safe for you to appear in public.

No one can be in the lead who is unwilling to remain in the background, and no one can govern with safety who does not know how to obey. No one is truly happy who is aware of an unclean conscience.

3. Even the assurance of the Saints was always mingled with the fear of God. Although they excelled in virtue, yet they were careful to be humble and diligent in the service of God. On the contrary, the assurance of the wicked comes from their pride and presumption, and in the end deceives them.

Therefore, never be sure of yourself in this life, whether you are religious or secular. Often those who have enjoyed the esteem of others are in grave danger because they are overconfident.

4. It is a good thing that many of us are not free of temptations, for these make us watchful so that we do not become proud and rely upon worldly consolation.

What a clear conscience we would have if we stopped running after passing pleasures and meddling in worldly affairs! What serenity we would have if we would do away with vain distractions and, thinking only of the things of God and our salvation, put all our confidence in Him.

5. Unless we have sincere repentance, we are not worthy to receive spiritual consolation. If you are truly penitent, seek the quiet of your room and shut out the noise of the world, for it is written: *"Be careful not to sin; reflect in silence as you lie upon your beds"* (Ps 4:5). There you will find the grace that you may easily lose outside.

A room you live in becomes dear to you, while if you are seldom in it, you will grow tired of it. If in the beginning of your conversion you are often in it, afterward you will find it to be a dear friend and a real comfort.

6. In silence and stillness the devout soul advances and learns the hidden truths of Scripture. There it finds the salutary tears that wash away the guilt of sin, so that it grows more intimate with God as it severs itself from the clamor of the world. The more you keep away from friends and acquaintances, the more our Lord and His Angels will draw near to you.

It is better to lead a solitary life and to look to the welfare of your soul, than to work miracles and neglect yourself. It is praiseworthy for a devout person seldom to go out, to avoid being seen and to have no desire for the company of others.

7. Why do you long to see that which you are forbidden to have? *The world with all its deceitful pleasures soon passes* (1 Jn 2:17). Sensuality lures you abroad, but when the time is past, you only return home with a remorseful conscience and a heavy heart.

Often a glad going forth is followed by a sad return; and a joyous evening causes a heavy morning. This is so with earthly joys, which begin pleasantly, but end only in disaster.

What can you see elsewhere that you cannot see here? The earth and sky and all the elements of which all earthly things are made! What can you see elsewhere that will endure long under the sun? If all the world could pass before your eyes at one time, what would it be but an empty vision?

8. Lift up your eyes to God in heaven and beg His forgiveness for your sins. Abandon idle things to idle minds and concern yourself only with what is God's will for you. Close your door and call to your beloved Jesus. Remain with Him in your room, opening your heart completely to Him; for nowhere else will you find so much peace.

If only you had never left your room or listened to idle rumors, you would have remained in peace of mind; but as often as you take pleasure in hearing the latest news, then you must suffer the consequences of a troubled mind and heart.

CHAPTER 21

On Compunction of Heart

IF YOU want to make progress, keep your soul in the fear of God and never wish to be completely free. Discipline your senses and never indulge in hilarity.

Have sorrow for your sins and you will find interior peace. Repentance opens the way to many blessings, which dissipation soon destroys.

2. It is a wonder that any of us can be wholly contented in this life when we think of our exile from God and of the daily dangers our soul faces. But because of frivolity and the negligence of our defects we are unaware of the misery of our own soul. Often we laugh when we ought to weep, for there is no perfect freedom nor real joy except in the fear of God and in a good conscience.

Those are truly happy who have the grace to rid themselves of temptation to distractions and turn to God by sincere contrition. Those, too, are happy who avoid the things that only give them a troubled conscience.

Fight hard against your sins; bad habits are overcome by good habits. Do not make excuses that others hinder you; for if you let them alone, they will let you alone to do what you must.

3. Do not mind other people's business and do not become involved in the affairs of great persons. Keep an eye on your own self and reprove yourself rather than your friends. Do not be upset if you are not in the favor of the worldly-minded; but rather be sorry that your behavior is not that of a devout servant of God.

It is far better for a person to lack consolations in this life, particularly those of the flesh. If we receive little or no spiritual consolations it is our own fault (though sometimes the lack of them is a test of our faith); for we do not have true compunction of heart, nor do we refrain altogether from seeking consolations from without.

4. Realize that you are unworthy of supernatural consolation, but instead deserve tribulation. The comforts of the world are distasteful to those who have perfect contrition for their sins.

Good people always find enough reason to have sorrow and to weep; for whether they look at themselves or think about their neighbor, they realize that no one lives in this world free from affliction; and the more thoroughly they look into their own hearts, the deeper will be their sorrow. But the cause for real grief and contrition is the remembrance of our sins, in which we are so enmeshed that we can hardly think about spiritual matters.

5. If you would think more often about death than of a long life, you would be more eager to amend your life. If you thought seriously about the pains of hell or purgatory, you would gladly endure pain and labor, and no hardship would seem too much for you. But since these things do not penetrate the heart and we still love the false pleasures of this world, we tend to be cold and indifferent.

It is this weakness of the spirit that often makes our wretched bodies complain for the slightest reason. Therefore, humbly pray to God, that in His merciful goodness He will give you the spirit of penance, and in the words of the Prophet say to Him: Feed me, O Lord, *"with the bread of tears"* and give me *"tears to drink beyond measure"* (Ps 80:6).

CHAPTER 22

On the Consideration of Human Misery

YOU ARE wretched wherever you are and no matter which way you turn—unless your turning is to God. Why are you easily upset just because things do not go your way?

Who is there that gets his or her own way all the time? Neither you, nor I, nor anybody; for there is no one in this world without troubles or difficulties whether that person is a king or the Pope. Who is best off? Only the one who is willing to suffer something for the love of God.

2. But there are many spiritually weak people who say to themselves: "Look at what a nice life those people lead! They are rich and powerful, are highly regarded by others, and hold good positions in life." Yet if you look at the rewards of heaven, you will see how little these earthly things count; in fact, they can become a burden, for they require constant care and you never know when you may lose them.

Our happiness does not consist in many possessions; enough for our needs is sufficient. Our life on earth is a trial, and the more spiritual we become, the more painful it is, for we better understand the defects of human corruption. Even to eat, drink, sleep, wake, rest, work and care for the other needs of the body brings misery to a devout person, who longs to be rid of bodily cares and the bondage of sin.

3. For the spiritual person is weighed down by bodily necessities in this world. That is why the Prophet longed to be freed from these necessities, praying: *"From my necessities, set me free, O Lord"* (Ps 25:17—Vulgate). But woe to them who do not realize their misery, and still worse for those who love this miserable and corruptible life; for there are those who are so in love with it that even if they had to earn their living by hard labor or by begging, they would never want to leave it for the kingdom of God.

4. O foolish and senseless people, who are so deeply entrenched in material things as to have no feeling or desire except for the pleasures of the flesh! When death comes, then they will realize how utterly worthless were the things they loved so much.

But the holy Saints and the faithful friends of Christ did not cater to what gratified the flesh nor to what was pleasing to the world. They set their sights and placed all their hopes on eternal joys, for fear that loving visible things might draw them downward.

5. O my brother or sister, do not lose your desire for spiritual progress while time and opportunity still await you! Why do you delay any

longer? Get up; now is the time to begin! Say to yourself: "Now is the time for good works, now is the time to fight, now is the time to make reparation for the sins of the past."

When you are troubled, that is the best time for you to merit. Yes, you must pass through fire and water before you come to the place of refreshment. Unless you gain full control of yourself, you will never overcome sin, and life will always be a burden because of the frailty of our nature.

Gladly would we be freed from all sin and misery, but because we have lost our innocence by sin, we have lost true happiness as well. We must wait in patience, therefore, having confidence in the mercy of God, until iniquity passes away and death is swallowed up in life eternal.

6. How frail is human nature that we are always inclined to evil! Today you confess your sins and tomorrow you commit the same ones again. Now you resolve to be vigilant, with all good intention to persevere, and shortly after you act as if you never had a good intention.

We have good reason to humble ourselves and never to have a good opinion of ourselves, since we are so weak and unstable. The virtue we strove by grace to gain may soon be lost through carelessness.

7. What will become of us in the end when we relax our efforts so soon? Woe to us if we take life easy now—as though our eternity were assured— when in reality there is no sign of true holiness in our conduct!

It would be helpful for us to begin over again and be instructed in the way of perfection. Perhaps then there may be hope of future amendment and progress in the spiritual life.

CHAPTER 23

Meditation on Death

THE HOUR of death will soon come for you. See to it that you spend your time here well. There is a common saying that human beings are here today and gone tomorrow. And once they are out of sight, they are soon forgotten.

How dull we are and hard of heart, for we think only of the present and make little provision for the life hereafter! If you were wise, you would so order your life as though you were to die before the day is over.

If your conscience were clear, you would not be afraid of death. Better to give up sin than to fear death. If you are unprepared to face death today, how will you be tomorrow? Tomorrow is uncertain and you may not be here to see it.

2. What good is a long life if we do not use it to advance spiritually? Sad to say, it often happens that a long life adds to our guilt and not to our amendment. If only we could point to one day in our life that was really well spent! Many count the years of their conversion, but often there is little to show for it.

If it is frightening to die, it may be more dangerous to live long. You are truly blessed if you keep the hour of your death before you and prepare yourself for it. If you ever saw anyone die, remember that you too must travel the same path.

3. In the morning think that you may not live till night; and when night comes, do not be sure that you will live till tomorrow. Therefore always be ready, and so live that you will not have an unprovided death.

Many have died suddenly and without warning; *for the Son of Man will come at an hour when you least expect Him* (Lk 12:40). When the hour of death comes, you will begin to think differently about your past life and great will be your sorrow then that you have been so negligent and lazy in God's service.

4. How happy and wise are those who try now to become what they would want to be at the hour of death. A perfect contempt of the world, an ardent desire to progress in virtue, a love of discipline, a prompt obedience, a denial of self and a patient bearing of all adversities for the love of Christ will give you great confidence of dying happily.

Strive to do good deeds while you are well, for when you are sick you do not know what you will be able to do. Sickness does not often change us for the better. Also, few are sanctified by making many pilgrimages.

5. Do not put your trust in your friends and neighbors, nor put off the care of your soul's welfare until after death, for you will be forgotten sooner than you think. It is better to provide for

your salvation now by doing good deeds that will earn eternal merit for you than to rely on the help of others after your death. If you have no concern for yourself now, who will be concerned about you later on?

Time is precious now, and now is the day of salvation, the acceptable time. But alas, that you spend the time so unprofitably! The time will come when you will wish that you had one more day—even one hour—to put your life in order, but there is no assurance that you will get it.

6. O my dear friend, from how great a peril may you now deliver yourself and from what terrible fear, if only you would dread to offend God in this life and always be ready for death! Learn to live now that at the hour of death you may rather rejoice than tremble.

If you will have a life with Christ, you must learn how to die to the world, and if you are to go freely to Christ, then you must learn now to despise all things. Chastise your body now by penance, so that you can face death with sure confidence that God will forgive you.

7. You are a fool if you think you have a long life ahead when you are not sure of living even one day. How many have been deceived with thinking they had a long life ahead and have died without warning.

How often have you heard that someone was murdered, another drowned and still another fell and broke his neck; how this person choked to death and another dropped dead while at play?

PRELUDES TO THE LAST JUDGMENT—"Following that distress, the sun will be darkened, and the moon will not give forth its light, and the stars will be falling from the sky, and the heavenly powers will be shaken" (Mk 13:24f).

Some have burned to death; some were killed by guns, others by disease, and still others at the hands of robbers.

One thing is certain: death is the end of all! A person's life passes suddenly like a shadow.

8. How many people will remember you and pray for you once you are dead? So do all you can now, for you do not know when you will die or what you will face after death. Gain merit for eternity now while there is time and concern yourself only with your eternal salvation.

Attend to those things that are to God's honor and glory. Honor the Saints and follow their example and you will have friends waiting *to receive you into everlasting dwellings* (Lk 16:9) when your life here is ended.

9. Live on earth as a pilgrim and a stranger, unconcerned with the world's business. Let your heart remain free and lifted up to God, for you have not here a lasting city. Persevere in prayer, sending your aspirations daily up to God, so that at the hour of death your soul may depart from this world and go to its Lord.

CHAPTER 24

On the Last Judgment and the Punishment for Sins

IN ALL things look to the end and how you will appear before the strict Judge. Nothing is hidden from Him; neither will He accept bribes, nor receive excuses. He will judge all things rightly and truly.

Wretched sinner that you are, what answer will you then give your God, Who knows all your evil deeds, when here you are afraid to face an angry human being? Why do you not provide for that day of judgment now, since there will be no one to defend or make excuses for you, for everyone will have enough to do to answer for oneself? Now you can gain merit; your tears and sighs are heard and your sorrow and repentance acceptable.

2. Patient persons have a wholesome purgatory in this world, who, enduring the wrong of another, are more concerned with the sin committed than with the injury done to them. They will pray willingly for their enemies and from their hearts forgive those who offend them; they are quick to ask others for forgiveness; they are more easily moved to compassion than to anger; and putting restraint upon themselves, they resist sin and bring their bodies under subjection.

It is better to get rid of sins now, doing away with your bad habits, than to wait to have them purged hereafter. We truly deceive ourselves by our unrestrained self-love.

3. What will the eternal fires devour but your sins? The more you spare yourself now and the more you give in to the clamors of the flesh, the more bitterly will you regret it hereafter and the more fuel you will store up for those fires.

Persons shall be punished most for those sins in which they have offended most. The slothful will be pricked with red-hot spikes; the gluttons will be tormented with great hunger and thirst.

The lovers of luxury and dissipation will be immersed in sulphur and burning pitch and the envious will wail and howl like mad dogs.

4. No sin will be without its proper punishment. For the proud person will be filled with shame and confusion and the covetous will waste away in poverty and need. One hour of pain there will be more grievous than a hundred years spent in rigorous penance here. There is no rest or comfort for the damned. Sometimes here we have periods of rest from work and the consolation of our friends.

Be sorry for your sins now so that on the day of judgment you may be secure in the company of the blessed. Then shall the just stand with great constancy against those who have persecuted and oppressed them. Then those who humbly submitted themselves to human judgments shall take their stand as judges. Great will be the confidence of the poor and the humble, while the proud will tremble with dread.

5. Then those will appear to have been wise in this world who contented themselves to be taken for fools and despised for the sake of Christ. They will be glad that they suffered tribulation patiently in this world, for all iniquity shall stop its mouth.

Every devout person shall be joyful, while the irreligious will be sad. The flesh that was chastised shall exult more than if it had been pampered with luxuries. The shabby garment shall shine and the fine clothing look like rags.

The poor dwelling shall be more celebrated than the gilded palace, constant patience shall help more than all worldly power, and simple obedience shall be rated higher than all worldly cunning.

6. Then a good clean conscience will make you happier than all the philosophy you have learned and your contempt of riches will be of more value than all the treasures in the world. You will have more consolation for your devout praying than all the feasts you could have enjoyed.

You will be happier for having kept silence than for all the long talks and the gossip; good deeds will be of greater value than clever words; and a disciplined life and hard penance will be more pleasing than all the pleasures of earth.

Therefore, learn to suffer small trials now in order to be saved from greater ones. Better to try here what you may have to suffer hereafter.

And if you can endure so little pain now, how will you stand everlasting torments? If you lose your patience over a small suffering now, what will the fires of hell do hereafter? You cannot have two heavens: it is impossible to enjoy yourself here and afterward to reign with Christ.

7. If you had lived your whole life up to now in honors and pleasures, what good would it do you if suddenly you were to die now? Therefore, all is vanity except loving and serving God. Those who love God with their whole hearts need not fear death or punishment, judgment or hell; for perfect love is a sure path to God. But if people

still delight in sin, it is no wonder that they fear both death and hell.

It is good, however, that although love is not perfect enough to withdraw you from evil, at least the fear of hell restrains you. Those who set aside the fear of God will not persevere long in the state of grace, but will soon fall into the snares of the devil.

CHAPTER 25

On the Fervent Amendment of Our Whole Life

BE ALERT and diligent in the service of God, thinking often why you were born and why you have left the world. Was it not that you should live only for God and become a spiritual person? Certainly it was.

Therefore, set your heart on striving for perfection, for shortly you will be rewarded for all your labors and after that you will never experience sorrow and dread.

Your labor will last but a short time and then you will receive everlasting rest and peace. If you are faithful and fervent in doing good, there is no doubt that God will be faithful and generous in His reward.

Have a firm hope that you will attain the victory; but do not presume on this, for then there is danger of your becoming careless and proud.

2. Once there was a person who was anxious whether or not he was in the state of grace; one day in his sadness, he fell to his knees before an altar in the church, praying: "Oh, if only I knew whether I would persevere to the end of my life!"

Suddenly he heard a voice within him, answering: "What would you do if you did know? Do now what you would do then and you will be secure."

Immediately he was comforted and commended himself entirely to God's will and all his doubts ceased. After that, he never speculated as to what would become of him.

Instead he applied himself to know what was the will of God for him and how he might begin and end all his good works to the honor and glory of God.

3. The Prophet David tells us: *"Put your trust in the Lord and do good, that you may dwell in the land and be secure"* (Ps 37:3). One thing holds many back from spiritual advancement and earnest amendment, and that is the fear and dislike of the effort and difficulties involved in the struggle.

Yet those attain surpassing virtue who struggle bravely against the very things which they find hardest and most repugnant to them. For a person profits most and gains the most graces precisely in the area where the difficulties are greatest and require the most mortification.

4. Certain it is that all persons do not have the same difficulties to overcome and mortify. Nevertheless, those who ardently love God, even though their passions are stronger than those of others, will be better able to grow in virtue than those with good habits and fewer passions, but who are less fervent in pursuing holiness.

Two things which you need to make real progress are: you must withdraw yourself from those things to which you are prone by nature and strive for the particular virtue you most need. Especially be on your guard against and correct those faults which most annoy you in other people.

5. Use all occasions for your spiritual gain. If you observe good example, follow it; and if you see bad example, take care not to do the same; if you have already fallen into this fault, work to correct it quickly. As your eye observes others, be sure that you also are observed by them.

What an inspiration to see religious persons devout and fervent in the love of God, courteous and self-disciplined!

On the other hand, how sad to see those whose lives are disorderly and who do not practice those things to which they are called. How detrimental it is for us to neglect the purpose of our calling and to divert our minds to things that are not our concern.

6. Keep in mind your commitment. Place yourself before the image of Christ Crucified and see if you are not ashamed, when looking into His life, that you have done so little to model your life on His.

Those who will meditate devoutly on the life and passion of our Lord will find there all that is necessary for them and will not have to look further. If Jesus Crucified were often in our hearts, how quickly we would learn all things we need to know!

7. Religious persons put up with and accept willingly whatever they are commanded to do; but the neglectful and lukewarm are always in difficulty and have great anguish besides, for they lack interior comfort and cannot seek it outside.

Undisciplined persons, who seek to be released from their duties, will always be in trouble, for nothing will ever satisfy them.

8. Consider the strict life others lead who are bound by the rules of the cloister. They seldom go out, live in retirement, eat sparingly, are poorly clothed, work hard, speak little, keep long vigils, rise early, pray much, read often and discipline themselves.

Look how the Carthusians, Cistercians and many other religious men and women rise in the night to sing the Divine Office! Aren't you ashamed, then, of being so lazy and lukewarm!

9. What a beautiful life it would be if we had nothing else to do but lift our hearts and voices to praise our Lord! If you never had to eat, drink or sleep, but were solely occupied in praising God and studying the way of perfection, you would be far happier than you are now when there is always some bodily need to be looked after.

If only there were not such needs and we could be wholly occupied with spiritual refreshment which, sad to say, we taste all too seldom!

10. When people reach that state where they seek consolation from no creature, then they begin to taste the sweetness of God and to be content with whatever happens.

They care for no worldly profit, however great, nor pine for the want of it, because they are wholly committed to God, Who is their all—God for Whom nothing is ever lost or dies and to Whom all things live and ever obediently serve Him.

11. Always remember your end and that time lost can never be regained. Without applying yourself diligently, you will never acquire virtue. The moment you begin to be lukewarm, your trouble begins.

But, if you give yourself wholeheartedly to fervor, you will experience great help from God and you will find the pursuit of virtue less burdensome than you did at first.

Those who are fervent and loving will always be ready to do God's will. It is harder to resist vices and passions than to toil and sweat in bodily labors.

If you do not shun little faults, you will gradually fall into greater ones. If you spent the day well, you will be happy when night comes.

Watch yourself, stir yourself up, warm yourself; whatever your obligation to others, do not neglect your own soul. The more restraints you put on yourself, the more spiritual progress you will make and the greater your attachment to the will of God.

JESUS GIVES US PEACE IN THE SPIRIT—"The Advocate, the Holy. Spirit, Whom the Father will send in My Name, will teach you everything and remind you of all that I have said to you. Peace I leave with you, My peace I give to you" (Jn 14:26f).

BOOK 2

CONSIDERATIONS FOR LEADING AN INTERIOR LIFE

CHAPTER 1

On Interior Conversation

OUR LORD says: *"The kingdom of God is in your midst"* (Lk 17:21). The only way your soul will find rest is to turn to God with your whole heart and abandon this wretched world. Learn to despise exterior things and give your attention to the inner things; then you will see the kingdom of God come within you.

The kingdom of God *means peace and joy in the Holy Spirit* (Rom 14:17), which is denied to evil people. Our Lord will visit the devout with His consolations, if they will make room for Him in the depths of their hearts. This is where He desires to be, and He will bring them many graces and much peace, and the sublime intimacy of His presence.

2. Lose no time, then, faithful soul, in preparing your heart to meet Christ, the Beloved, so that He may come and live in you. Does He not

say: "*Whoever loves Me will keep My word, . . . We will come to him and make Our abode with him*" (Jn 14:23)? Therefore, make room for Him in your heart and shut out all others.

If you have Christ, you are rich indeed, for only He can fill all your needs. He will be your provider and defender and your faithful helper in every need, so that you need not trust in any other.

How quickly people change and fail us; but *Christ abides forever* (Jn 12:34) and remains at our side to the end.

3. No confidence is to be placed in mortal human beings, no matter how helpful they may be or how dear to us, for we are all frail. Neither should you be downcast if one day they are on your side and the next day they are against you; for humans are changeable like the wind.

Therefore, put your complete trust in God and let Him be the center of your love and fear. He will answer for you and will do what He sees best for you.

What are you but an alien and a pilgrim! Only if you are united to Christ will you have a rest.

4. Why do you look to have rest on this earth when it is not your true home? Your home is heaven, and all earthly things are transitory and you as well. Do not cling to them, for you will become enmeshed in them and be destroyed. Direct your thoughts upward to God, and all your prayer to Christ continually.

If you are unable to contemplate the Godhead, then let your thoughts dwell on the Passion of Christ, finding in those sacred wounds a home. If you fly to the wound in Christ's side, you will find comfort in all your troubles. You will not care then if others despise you, and will easily bear up under criticism.

5. When our Lord lived on earth He was looked down upon by people, and in the hour of His greatest need, He was left by His friends to bear insults and shame.

Can you dare to complain when Christ was so willing to suffer and be despised? Do you expect all to be your friends and patrons, when Christ was surrounded by enemies and slanderers?

If all goes well with you on earth, how can you expect to be crowned in heaven for a patience you never practiced? How can you be Christ's friend if you will not be opposed? Therefore, you must suffer with Christ and for Christ, if you want to reign with Him.

6. If once you had entered into the interior of Jesus and there tasted a little of His ardent love, you would not consider your own convenience or inconvenience, but would even rejoice over insults done to you; for love of Jesus would urge you to despise yourself.

Those who love Jesus and the truth, who lead an interior life free from unruly affections, can turn to God at will, lift themselves up in spirit and repose in Christ with joy.

7. They are wise who observe things as they are and not by what is said about them, or by the value put on them; for they are taught by God and not by humans.

Those who can raise their minds to God, with little regard to outward things, do not need to look for place or time to pray or to do good deeds.

For interior persons, not being wholly occupied with the things of sense, can easily fix their minds on God. Their exterior work is no obstacle to them, nor is any necessary employment; they will apply themselves to each in turn and refer all to the will of God.

If your soul is well disposed and disciplined, you will not be surprised or disturbed by the perverse conduct of others. You will be hindered and distracted to the extent that you are taken up with worldly matters.

8. If you were well purified from worldly attachments, whatever happened would turn to your spiritual profit and to an increase of grace and virtue in your soul. But because of your excess love of earthly things, many things displease and annoy you.

Nothing so defiles and ensnares a person's heart as the undisciplined love of created things. If you will refuse outward consolations, then you will think of heavenly things and continually give praise to Him with a joyful heart.

CHAPTER 2

On Humble Submission

DO NOT be concerned about who is on your side or who is against you; just be sure that God is with you. If your conscience is clear, be sure that He will defend you. The malice of others can never harm you as long as He is by your side.

Be silent and endure for a while and you will experience the help of God in your need. No doubt about it, for God knows when and how to deliver you. So put yourself in His care. It is up to God to help and to deliver from all dilemma. However, we should realize that often it is good for others to know our defects and call us to order for them, for it keeps us humble.

2. When you admit your faults, you easily pacify others and reconcile yourself with those you have offended. God never refuses the humble; rather He delivers and comforts them and fills them with His grace. He also opens to them the secrets of His Heart and draws them to Himself, raising them to the heights of glory because of their humility.

Humble people are always at peace, even when they are put to shame, because they trust in God and not in the world. So, if you wish to reach the height of perfection, never think of yourself as being virtuous until you know sincerely in your heart that you are the least of all.

CHAPTER 3

The Peaceful Person

YOU MUST first have peace in your own soul before you can make peace between other people. Peaceable people accomplish more good than learned people do. Those who are passionate often can turn good into evil and readily believe the worst. But those who are honest and peaceful turn all things to good and are suspicious of no one.

The discontented are easily troubled; they never know a quiet moment, nor will they leave others at rest. Many times they say the wrong thing and miss the chance of doing good. They are great for saying what others should do, but neglect their own duties. Begin by looking to your soul and then you will be better able to have zeal for your neighbor.

2. You are always ready and able to excuse yourself, putting the best possible construction on your own actions, but you refuse to listen to the excuses of others. The charitable way is to accuse yourself and to excuse your neighbor. If you want others to bear with you, then you must bear with them.

Look at yourself and see how far you are from real charity and humility, which cannot be resentful against anyone but oneself. It is no test of virtue to be on good terms with easy-going people, for they are always well liked. And, of course, all of us want to live in peace and prefer those who agree with us.

But the real test of virtue and deserving of praise is to live at peace with the perverse, or the aggressive and those who contradict us, for this needs a great grace.

3. There are some contented people who can live peaceably with others; and some there are who can neither have peace themselves nor leave others in peace. They are a cross to others, but a heavier cross to themselves. There are also some who can remain at peace themselves and seek to establish peace among others.

However, in this mortal life, our peace consists in the humble bearing of suffering and contradictions, not in being free of them, for we cannot live in this world without adversity. Those who can best suffer will enjoy the most peace, for such persons are masters of themselves, lords of the world, with Christ for their friend, and heaven as their reward.

CHAPTER 4

On Purity of Mind and a Simple Intention

WE ARE lifted up above earthly things by two wings: simplicity and purity. Simplicity regulates the intentions and purity the affections. Simplicity looks to God and purity finds Him and savors Him. No good work will hinder you if your heart is free from inordinate affections; on the contrary, you will grow in the way of perfection.

If your main object is the will of God and the good of your neighbor, you will have great interior freedom. If your heart is straight with God, then every creature will be a mirror of life and a book of heavenly teaching. There is no creature so insignificant and small which does not reflect the goodness of God.

2. If you had a heart that was good and pure you would see all things clearly and understand them well. A clean heart penetrates both heaven and hell. As people are inwardly, so do they judge outward things.

If there is any true joy in this world, only the person with a clean conscience possesses it. And wherever there is misery and affliction, the evil conscience experiences it best. Iron cast into the fire loses its rust and becomes clean and bright; and those who make God the center of their lives are cleansed of slothfulness and are changed into new persons.

The moment you begin to grow lukewarm, everything is a big effort and you willingly receive distractions from without. But as soon as you begin to conquer yourself and walk uprightly in the way of God, then the effort expended seems little which before you thought was insurmountable.

CHAPTER 5

On Knowing Yourself

WE CANNOT count on ourselves much, for often through lack of grace and understanding our judgment is a limited one and we soon lose what we have through our own neglect. Often we are unaware of our own interior blindness. Many times we do evil and, what is far worse, we justify it.

Sometimes our passions rule us and we mistake it for zeal. We are critical of the small defects in our neighbors, but overlook the serious faults in ourselves.

We are quick to complain of what we put up with from others, with never a thought of what others suffer from us.

If we would see ourselves as we really are, we would not find cause to judge others severely.

2. Those who are turned to God consider the care of themselves before all other cares; and looking seriously to themselves, they find it easy to be silent about the deeds of others.

You will never be an interior person and a follower of Christ unless you learn not to meddle in the affairs of others and to look to your own.

If you are concerned wholly with God and yourself, you will be unconcerned with what goes on around you. Where are you when you are not recollected? And when you have been busy with other people's affairs, what have you to show for it if you have neglected yourself?

If, therefore, you wish to have peace in your soul and to be united to God, set aside all else and focus the eye of your soul on your own deeds.

3. If you want to advance spiritually, keep yourself free from temporal anxieties. You will only lose ground if you set any value on material things.

Consider nothing great, nothing acceptable to you, unless it be God Himself, or of God.

Whatever comfort you derive from any creature counts as nothing.

Those who love God and their own soul for the love of God despise all else; for only the infinite and eternal God can fill our every need and desire, the solace of our soul and the true joy of our heart.

CHAPTER 6

On the Joy of a Good Conscience

THE glory of a good person is the evidence of a good conscience. Have a good conscience and you will always be happy.

A good conscience can bear a great deal and still remain serene in the midst of adversity, while a bad conscience is fearful and easily ruffled.

Only be glad when you have done well. Evil persons are never really happy, nor do they feel peace within them; for *"there is no peace for the wicked, says the Lord"* (Isa 48:22).

Even though the wicked may protest that peace is theirs and that no evil shall harm them, do not believe them. For God's wrath will suddenly overtake them, and all they have done will be brought to nothing and their plans destroyed.

2. Those who love God will glory in tribulation, for their only joy is to glory in the cross of Jesus Christ, our Lord. The glory given and received by humans lasts but a little while and usually it is followed by sadness.

The glory of good persons is in their own consciences, not in the praise of others. The happiness of the good is in God and of God and their joy is in the truth.

Those who long for true everlasting happiness do not care for that which is temporal. Those who seek temporal glory and do not treat it with contempt have little love for the joy of heaven. Those who are indifferent to praise or blame have great tranquility of heart.

3. Persons whose conscience is clear have peace and contentment. You are no better for being praised, nor worse for being blamed, for you are what you are, nor will you be more nor less than God sees you to be. If you know what you are within yourself, the opinion of others will not interest you.

We see only the face, but God sees into the heart (1 Sam 16:7). We look at the actions, but God considers the intentions.

Always to do the best you can and to make little of yourself is the mark of a humble soul. To refuse consolation from any creature shows cleanness of heart and confidence in God.

4. Those who seek no outward testimony for themselves have committed themselves entirely to God. For St. Paul says: *"For it is not the one who commends himself who is really approved, but the one whom the Lord commends"* (2 Cor 10:18). Those who continually live intimately with God, not bound by any outward attachment, are in the state of an interior life.

CHAPTER 7

On the Love of Jesus above All Things

HOW BLESSED are those who know how good it is to love Jesus and to despise themselves for His sake. Jesus wills to be loved alone above all other things and we must forsake all other loves but His.

The love of creatures deceives and fails, but Jesus' love is ever faithful and enduring. Those who cling to creatures will fall with them; but those who always cling to Jesus will stand firm forever.

Love Him and keep Him for your friend; for when all others forsake you, He will not leave you nor let you perish in the end. Sooner or later you must be separated from all creatures, whether you will it or not.

2. Remain close to Jesus in life and in death, committing yourself to His faithful keeping. When all others fail you, He will help you. However, your Beloved is of such a nature that He will not accept a divided heart; but will have it for Himself alone and will reign there as a king on his throne.

If only you could empty your heart of every creature, how gladly would Jesus come and dwell with you. All those other things in which you placed your trust besides Jesus, you can consider as almost a complete loss. *"All flesh is grass, and all its glory shall fade like the flower of the field"* (Isa 40:6).

TRUSTING LOVE FOR GOD—"Gaze upon the birds in the sky . . . your heavenly Father feeds them. . . . Let your main focus be on His kingdom and His righteousness, and all these things will be given to you as well" (Mt 6:26, 33).

3. If you only observe outward appearances, you will soon be deceived; and if you seek consolation or benefit from others, more often than not you will suffer loss. But if in all things you look to Jesus, you will most certainly find Him.

To seek yourself is to find yourself—but to your own destruction. If you do not seek your Lord, you do more harm to yourself than do all worldly temptations and all your enemies.

CHAPTER 8

On the Familiar Friendship of Jesus

WHEN our Lord is present, all goes well and nothing seems hard to do for His love; but when He is absent, everything is difficult. When Jesus does not speak to our soul, no other consolation suffices; but if He speaks only one word, we feel great inner joy.

Did not Mary Magdalene get up at once from where she sat weeping as soon as Martha told her: *"The Teacher is here and is asking for you"* (Jn 11:28)? Certainly she did. How happy the hour when Jesus calls us from our tears to spiritual joy!

How dry and hard of heart you are without Jesus and how foolish and useless for you to desire anything besides Jesus, for that desire can harm you more than if you should lose the whole world! For what can the world give you without Jesus?

2. To be without Jesus is the torment of hell, but to be with Him is the joy of paradise. If you have Jesus there is nothing an enemy can do to you.

Those who find Jesus find the pearl of great price—indeed, the highest good; but those who lose Him lose all. They are in dire poverty who live without Jesus; but they are richest who live with Him.

3. It is a great art to know how to talk with Jesus, and to know how to keep Him with you is great wisdom. Be humble and peaceful and Jesus will be with you; be devout and quiet and He will stay with you.

But as soon as you turn back to outward things, you will quickly drive away your Lord and lose His grace. And if you drive Him from you, to whom then will you flee and to whom will you look for a friend? How can you lead a good life without a friend? If Jesus is not your most dear friend, you will be sad and forsaken.

How foolish, therefore, to put your trust or happiness in any other. It would be better to have the whole world against you than to hurt Jesus. Of all who are dear to you, let Jesus be your best beloved.

4. All others must be loved for Jesus' sake, but Jesus for Himself alone. Jesus Christ must be loved exclusively, for He alone is proved good and faithful above all other friends. For Him and in Him, you must love friends and foes alike, praying to Him for them, that all may come to know and love Him.

Never long for special affection or praise, for this is God's sole right, and there is none like Him. Also, do not desire another's exclusive affection, nor give that person yours; but just let Jesus be in you and in every good person.

5. Be pure and free of heart and do not become entangled with any creature. If you wish to be free and to experience the sweetness of the Lord, then you must be naked and bring a pure heart to God.

But you can only attain this if you are led by His grace; so that setting aside all else, you may become one with Him alone. When God's grace comes to any persons, they are made strong to do all things; and when it leaves them, they are poor and weak and left only as it were to the pain of bodily penances.

But if this happens to you, do not be dejected nor despair, but resign yourself to the will of God, bearing whatever happens to you for the glory of Christ. For after winter follows summer, after night the day, and after the storm fair weather.

CHAPTER 9

On the Want of All Comfort

IT IS not hard to despise human comfort when the comfort of God is present; but it is quite another thing—and very difficult—to be able to do without both human and divine comfort and be willing to endure this desolation of heart for the glory of God, seeking yourself in nothing, nor thinking of your own merit.

It is no test of virtue if you are happy and devout when grace comes to the soul, for this is the time desirable to all. Those who are carried by the grace of God ride safely. It is no wonder they feel no burden who are carried by the Almighty and led by the Sovereign Guide.

2. We are always glad for solace and comfort and want no part of tribulation and we do not easily cast aside self-love.

The holy martyr, St. Lawrence, overcame the world, together with the priest he served, because he scorned the delights of the world; and for the love of Christ, he humbly suffered to have Sixtus the Pope, whom he dearly loved, taken from him. So through the love of the Creator he overcame the love of others, choosing what pleased God instead of human comfort.

See that you also learn to part with some necessary thing and a beloved friend for the love of God. Do not be grieved when you are forsaken by a friend, knowing that someday we must be separated from one another.

3. Before they can win the victory over self, people must go through a considerable conflict with self and be able to give their whole heart to God.

When people rely on their own strength, they easily incline toward human consolation. But those who love Christ and earnestly pursue virtue do not fall back on such consolations; they are glad to endure hard labor and discipline for Christ.

4. However, when God sends you spiritual comfort, accept it gladly and thank Him for it, but fully realize that it is God's mercy that sends it and not any deserving of yours. Do not be proud, presumptuous or overjoyed; rather let this gift humble you and be wary and fearful in all you do; for surely that time will pass away and be followed by temptation.

When consolation is withdrawn, do not be despondent, but humbly and patiently wait for the return of God; for He can give you back grace in fuller measure. Those who are experienced in the ways of God know that there is nothing new or strange about this, for such reverses were suffered by the Saints and the ancient Prophets.

5. There was one who in the time of grace said: *"In time of good fortune, I said, 'Nothing can ever sway me.'"* However, when grace was withdrawn he tells us how he felt: *"When You hid Your face, I was filled with terror."* Even then he did not despair, but earnestly implored the Lord: *"I will cry out to You, Lord, and call upon my God."* Finally, his prayer was answered and he was heard to say: *"The Lord listened and had mercy on me; the Lord became my helper."* In what way? *"You have turned my mourning into dancing,"* he says, *"and clothed me with joy"* (Ps 30:7-12).

If God has dealt this way with great Saints, then we who are so feeble must not be discouraged if sometimes we are fervent and other times cold, for the Holy Spirit comes and goes as He wills. That is why holy Job says: *"You examine him every morning and test him every hour of the day"* (Job 7:18).

6. In whom, then, can I hope, or in what may I place my trust, but in the great and endless mercy of God? For whether I am in the company of good persons, devout brothers and sisters or faithful friends; or whether I have holy books, excellent treatises, or beautiful chants and hymns, what good will they all do me when grace is withdrawn and I am left with poverty?

Patience is the best remedy in this state and the abandoning of self to the will of God.

7. I have never known anyone so religious and devout who has not sometimes had a withdrawal of grace or felt a diminishing of fervor. Never was a Saint so greatly enraptured or enlightened as not to be tempted at some time. For no persons are worthy of high contemplation unless they have suffered some tribulation for God.

Temptation going before is often a sign that consolation will follow. For to those who have been proved by temptation heavenly consolation is promised. *"To those who are victorious, I will give the right to eat from the tree of life"* (Rev 2:7).

8. God gives consolation to make us stronger in time of adversity. Then temptations follow to prevent us from becoming proud, thinking we are worthy of such a favor.

The devil never sleeps, neither is the flesh yet dead; therefore you must always be prepared to do battle, for you are surrounded by enemies that never rest.

CHAPTER 10

On Gratitude for God's Grace

WHY do you seek rest here when you are born to work? Dispose yourself to patience rather than to comfort and to carry the cross rather than to enjoyment. What temporal person would not gladly receive spiritual consolations if such a person could keep them always?

Spiritual consolations far surpass all worldly enjoyments and bodily pleasures. For all worldly delights are either empty or unclean; but spiritual joys alone are delightful and honest, since they spring from virtue and are instilled by God into a pure soul.

But no persons can enjoy these devout comforts for as long as they wish; for the time of temptation is never long absent.

2. False freedom of mind and over-self-confidence are a great hindrance to heavenly visits. God does well in sending the grace of comfort, but human beings do ill in not returning all to God with thanks. Therefore, these gifts of grace cannot flow in us because of our ingratitude to the Giver in not returning all to Him, the Source.

Grace is always given to the person who is grateful, and God readily gives to the humble what is taken from the proud.

3. I want no consolation that takes from me contrition, nor any contemplation that leads to presumption. All that is high in human eyes is not necessarily holy, nor is every desire pure, nor is everything dear to us always pleasing to God.

I gladly accept that grace which makes me more humble and prudent and more ready to deny myself. Those who have been taught by the gift of grace and chastened by the scourge of its withdrawal will not dare to think that any good comes by their own doing, and will openly confess that they are poor and naked.

Therefore, *give to God what is His* (Mt 22:21) and to yourself what is yours; that is, thank God for His graces and blame yourself for your sins, realizing that the punishment due to them is yours alone.

4. *Always set yourself in the lowest place* (Lk 14:10), and you will be given the highest; for the highest cannot exist without the lowest. The Saints who are highest in God's sight are the least in their own; and the more glorious they are, the more humble they are in heart, full of truth and heavenly joy and not desirous of vainglory.

Being grounded and confirmed in God, they can in no way be proud. They who ascribe to God whatever good they have received do not seek glory from one another, but only that glory which is from God; and the desire of their hearts is that God be praised in Himself and in all His Saints, and to this end they always tend.

5. Be grateful, therefore, for the least gift and you will be worthy to receive more. Regard the

least gift as the greatest and the most contemptible as a special prize. For if you consider the dignity of the Giver, no favor will seem small or valueless. Nothing is small that comes from the Most High God. Indeed, even if He sends punishment and affliction, we should accept it with gratitude; for whatever He permits to happen to us is always with our salvation in view.

If you desire to keep the grace of God, be thankful when it is given to you, patient when it is withdrawn. Pray that it may return; be humble and cautious that you do not lose it.

CHAPTER 11

On the Small Number of the Lovers of the Cross

JESUS has many lovers of His heavenly kingdom, but few cross-bearers. Many desire His consolation, but few His tribulation. Many will sit down with Him at table, but few will share His fast. All desire to rejoice with Him, but few will suffer for Him.

Many will follow Him to the breaking of the bread, but few will drink the bitter cup of His Passion. Many revere His miracles, but few follow the shame of His cross. Many love Jesus when all goes well with them, and praise Him when He does them a favor; but if Jesus conceals Himself and leaves them for a little while, they fall to complaining or become depressed.

2. They who love Jesus purely for Himself and not for their own sake bless Him in all trouble

and anguish as well as in time of consolation. Even if He never sent them consolation, they would still praise Him and give thanks.

3. Oh how powerful is the pure love of Jesus, when not mixed with self-interest or self-love! Are not they to be called hirelings who always look for comforts? And they who think only of their own advantage, do they not show themselves to be lovers of self rather than of Christ? Where will a person be found ready to serve God without looking for a reward?

4. It is hard to find anyone so spiritual who is willing to be stripped of all things. Where will you find a person truly poor in spirit and free from all attachment to creatures? Such a one is a *rare treasure brought from distant shores* (Prov 31:14).

If we were to give up all our possessions, it is still nothing; if we did severe penance, it is but little; if we acquired all knowledge, still are we far from virtue. Even if we had great virtue and fervent devotion, we would be lacking that one thing necessary above all else.

And what is that one thing? That leaving all things behind, we should leave self, renouncing our self completely and keeping nothing of self-love. And then when we have done all things that we know we ought to do, let us think that we have done nothing.

We should not regard as great that which may be considered so by others, but rather let us in truth look upon ourselves as worthless servants.

As our Lord, the Truth, has said: *"When you have done all you were ordered to do, say, 'We are unprofitable servants'"* (Lk 17:10). Then will we be truly poor in spirit and able to say with the Prophet: *"I am alone and afflicted"* (Ps 25:16). Yet there is no one richer or more powerful, no one more free than we are if we know how to renounce ourselves and all things, putting ourselves in the lowest place.

CHAPTER 12

On the Royal Road of the Cross

"ANYONE *who wishes to follow Me must deny self, take up the cross, and follow Me"* (Mt 16:24). Many think this is a hard saying; but it will be far harder if, on the day of judgment, a person hears those terrible words: *"Depart from Me, you accursed, into the eternal fire"* (Mt 25:41).

They who gladly accept and follow the word of the cross now will not then dread that sentence of eternal damnation. This sign of the cross shall appear in the heavens when our Lord comes to judge the world. Then all the servants of the cross, who made themselves like Christ Crucified, will go with great confidence before Christ, their Judge.

2. Why are you afraid to take up your cross, since it is the only way to the kingdom of heaven? In the cross is salvation and life; in the cross is

CHRIST'S COMING IN GLORY—"Then the sign of the Son of Man will appear in heaven, and all the peoples of earth will mourn, and they will see the Son of Man coming on the clouds of heaven with power and great glory" (Mt 24:30).

defense against our enemies. Through the cross heavenly sweetness is poured into our souls, our minds are strengthened and we experience spiritual joy.

In the cross is the height of virtue and the perfection of all sanctity. Without the cross there is no salvation for our souls, nor hope of life eternal. Take your cross, then, and follow Jesus, and you will go into everlasting life.

Remember that Jesus has gone before you bearing His cross and has given His life for you upon that cross, so that you may bear your own cross and long to die on it for love of Him. For if you die with Him, you will also live with Him; and if you have shared His suffering, you will also share His glory.

3. Behold how in the cross there is all and how all depends on our dying there; for there is no other way to life and interior peace except by way of the cross and by daily mortification. You can go anywhere you will, seek whatever you wish, but you will not find a higher road above nor safer road below than the road of the holy cross.

No matter how you plan things and arrange them to your liking, you still will find something to suffer, either willingly or unwillingly, and so you will always find the cross. Either you will suffer bodily pain, or you will endure in your soul tribulation of spirit.

4. Sometimes God will leave you to your own devices and sometimes your neighbor will irritate you; and what is worse, you will often be a trou-

ble to your own self. No remedy or comfort can free you from this affliction or make it easier for you to bear; you simply have to bear your cross as long as God wills it.

God wants you to learn to suffer tribulation without comfort and, submitting yourself entirely to Him, to grow in humility through tribulation. No one so deeply feels what Christ endured as one who has had to suffer as He did. The cross is always ready and waits everywhere for you; you cannot escape it no matter where you turn.

Wherever you go, you take yourself with you and you will always meet yourself face to face. Look upward or downward, within yourself or without; everywhere you will find the cross. And everywhere you must be patient if you desire interior peace and to merit a crown in heaven.

5. If you carry the cross willingly, it will carry you and bring you to your longed-for end, where there will be no more suffering—though this will not happen on earth. If you carry it grudgingly, it will become a burden and a heavier weight for you to carry, and yet you must bear it.

If you reject one cross, be sure that you will find another, perhaps heavier one.

6. Do you think you can escape that which no human being has been able to avoid? What Saint in this world was ever without the cross and without suffering?

Certainly our Lord, Jesus Christ, as long as He lived on earth, was never one hour without sorrow and anguish. *"Was it not necessary that the*

Messiah," He said, *"should suffer these things and so enter into His glory?"* (Lk 24:26). Then how can you seek any other road than this royal road, the road of the holy cross?

7. Christ's whole life was a cross and martyrdom; and do you expect pleasure and enjoyment for yourself? You make a grave mistake if you look for anything other than suffering; for this mortal life of ours is full of misery and surrounded with crosses.

The higher persons advance in the way of perfection, the heavier will they often find crosses to be. This is because the more their love of God grows, the more painful is their exile from God.

8. However, though such persons are afflicted in many ways, they do not lack entirely the relief of consolations; for they are aware of the great reward they reap by bearing their cross. And when they willingly submit themselves to it, their burden of suffering is turned into confidence that they will receive consolation from God.

The weaker the flesh becomes through affliction, the stronger the spirit is made by inward grace. And so it often happens that these persons gain so much strength through their desire of adversity and affliction in order to be conformed to the Crucified Christ, that they are unwilling to be without such sorrow and affliction. They are convinced that the more they can bear for love of Christ, the more pleasing they will be in God's eyes.

It is not by their own strength, but through the grace of Christ—which can and does have such a powerful effect on human frailty—that human beings can choose and even love that which by nature they hate and reject.

9. It is not the tendency of human beings to bear the cross and to love it, to chastise the body and to subdue it, to flee honors and to put up with reproaches, to despise themselves and to wish others to despise them, to bear all opposition and losses and not to desire any prosperity in this world.

If you trust in yourself, you will never accomplish this; but if you put your trust in God, you will be given strength from heaven, and the world and the flesh will be made subject to your command. If you are armed with faith and marked with the cross of Christ, you will not fear your enemy, the devil; for he will have no power over you.

10. Steel yourself, as a faithful servant of Christ, bravely to bear the cross of your Lord, Who out of love for you was nailed to the cross. Prepare yourself, then, to suffer all kinds of adversities and inconveniences in this wretched life; for you cannot avoid them no matter where you go, and they will find you no matter where you hide. So it is in life, and there is no avenue of escape but to keep yourself in patience.

If you desire to be our Lord's dear friend and to share what is His, then you must drink heartily of His chalice. As for consolations, leave those to His will and He will arrange them as He sees best for you.

But be you prepared to suffer tribulations and to consider them the greatest comforts, saying with St. Paul: *"I consider that the sufferings we presently endure are minuscule in comparison with the glory to be revealed in us"* (Rom 8:18), even though you alone were able to endure it all.

11. When you reach the degree of patience that tribulation is sweet to you and even relished for Christ, then you may trust that all is well with you, for you have found paradise on earth.

But as long as suffering plagues you and you seek to run away from it, then you will know that it is not well with you. You are a long way from perfect patience and the tribulation you flee will follow you everywhere.

12. If you resolve to do what you ought, that is, to suffer and to die to yourself, things will go better with you and you will find peace.

Even though you may have been caught up to the third heaven with St. Paul, you are not on that account free from adversity; for our Lord, speaking of St. Paul, said: *"I Myself will show him how much he will have to suffer for the sake of My Name"* (Acts 9:16). If you would love our Lord and serve Him constantly, then suffering remains your lot.

13. Oh that you were worthy to suffer something for the Name of Jesus! What great glory would await you, what great rejoicing among all the Saints, and, moreover, what great edification to your neighbor!

STATIONS
of the
CROSS

1. Jesus is Condemned to Death

O Jesus, help me to appreciate Your sanctifying grace more and more.

2. Jesus Bears His Cross

O Jesus, You chose to die for me. Help me to love You always with all my heart.

3. Jesus Falls the First Time

O Jesus, make me strong to conquer my wicked passions, and to rise quickly from sin.

4. Jesus Meets His Mother

O Jesus, grant me a tender love for Your Mother, who offered You for love of me.

STATIONS *of the* CROSS

5. Jesus is Helped by Simon

O Jesus, like Simon lead me ever closer to You through my daily crosses and trials.

6. Jesus and Veronica

O Jesus, imprint Your image on my heart that I may be faithful to You all my life.

7. Jesus Falls a Second Time

O Jesus, I repent for having offended You. Grant me forgiveness of all my sins.

8. Jesus Speaks to the Women

O Jesus, grant me tears of compassion for Your sufferings and of sorrow for my sins.

STATIONS *of the* CROSS

9. Jesus Falls a Third Time

O Jesus, let me never yield to despair. Let me come to You in hardship and spiritual distress.

10. He is Stripped of His Garments

O Jesus, let me sacrifice all my attachments rather than imperil the divine life of my soul.

11. Jesus is Nailed to the Cross

O Jesus, strengthen my faith and increase my love for You. Help me to accept my crosses.

12. Jesus Dies on the Cross

O Jesus, I thank You for making me a child of God. Help me to forgive others.

STATIONS *of the* CROSS

13. Jesus is Taken down from the Cross

O Jesus, through the intercession of Your holy Mother, let me be pleasing to You.

14. Jesus is Laid in the Tomb

O Jesus, strengthen my will to live for You on earth and bring me to eternal bliss in heaven.

Prayer after the Stations

JESUS, You became an example of humility, obedience and patience, and preceded me on the way of life bearing Your Cross. Grant that, inflamed with Your love, I may cheerfully take upon myself the sweet yoke of Your Gospel together with the mortification of the Cross and follow You as a true disciple so that I may be united with You in heaven. Amen.

All human beings commend patience, but how few there are who desire to suffer! You should be willing to suffer a little for Christ, since many suffer far greater things for the world.

14. Be sure of this, that you must lead a dying life; and the more you die to yourself here, the more you will begin to live to God. No one is worthy to understand heavenly things unless that person has first learned to bear afflictions for Christ.

Nothing is more pleasing to God, or more profitable for you, than to suffer gladly for Christ. And if you were given your choice, you should choose adversity rather than prosperity, for then you would become more like Christ and follow the example of the Saints. Our merit and progress in the spiritual life does not consist in the enjoyment of consolations and heavenly sweetness, but rather in bearing adversities and afflictions.

Had there been a better way than suffering for the good of a person's soul, our Lord would certainly have shown it by word and example. But since there was not, He clearly urged His disciples and all those who wished to follow Him to carry the cross, saying: *"Anyone who wishes to follow Me must deny self, take up the cross daily, and follow Me"* (Lk 9:23).

Therefore, when we have read and searched out all things, we come to the final conclusion, that *"It is necessary for us to undergo many hardships before we enter the kingdom of God"* (Acts 14:22). And may our Lord, Jesus Christ, bring us there.

JESUS INVITES US TO DIALOGUE WITH HIM—"I have called you friends, because I have revealed to you everything that I have heard from My Father. You did not choose Me. Rather, I chose you" (Jn 15:15f).

BOOK 3

ON INTERIOR CONVERSATION

CHAPTER 1

On the Way Christ Speaks Inwardly to the Soul

"I *WILL hear what the Lord God will speak within me*" (Ps 85:9), says a devout soul. Blessed is that soul who hears the Lord speaking within, and from His lips receives the words of comfort.

Blessed are the ears that heed the inner whisperings of the Lord, and pay no attention to the deceitful murmurings of this world; and blessed indeed are the ears which do not listen to the loud voices from outside, but instead are attentive to Him, Who inwardly teaches the truth. Blessed also are the eyes which are closed to things outside, but gaze intently on things within.

Blessed are they who acquire virtue and labor, by spiritual and corporal works, to receive daily more and more God's inward inspirations and teachings. They also are blessed who determine to serve God alone, ridding themselves of every hindrance from the world.

Listen, O my soul, to what has been said, and close the door of your senses that you may hear inwardly what the Lord Jesus speaks within your soul.

2. This is what your Beloved says: I am your salvation, your peace, and your life; keep close to Me, and in Me you will find peace. Abandon the love of passing things and seek those that are everlasting. What else are the things of time but deceptive? And how can any creature help you if your Lord abandons you?

Therefore, leaving all creatures and worldly things behind you, do your best to make yourself pleasing to Him, so that after this life you may come to life everlasting in the kingdom of heaven.

CHAPTER 2

How God Speaks within Us without Sound of Words

DISCIPLE: *Speak, Lord, for Your servant is listening* (1 Sam 3:9). *I am Your servant and beg You for the understanding to know Your commandments* (Ps 119:125). *Incline my heart to follow Your holy teachings* (Ps 119:36), *that they may seep into my soul as dew seeps into the grass* (Deut 32:2).

In ancient times the Israelites said to Moses: "*Speak to us yourself and we will listen; but do not have God speak to us or we will die*" (Ex 20:19).

But, Lord, this is not the way I pray; rather, with the Prophet Samuel, I humbly implore You: *speak, Lord, for Your servant is listening* (1 Sam 3:9).

Let not Moses nor any other Prophet speak to me, but only You, Lord, the inward inspirer and enlightener of all the Prophets. You alone can fully instruct me, whereas they, without You, will avail me nothing.

2. They may speak Your words, but they do not give the spirit to understand them. They utter beautiful language, but if You keep silence, my heart is not set on fire. They express the letter, but You reveal the meaning.

They lay mysteries before me, but You bring out the hidden meaning. They proclaim Your commandments, but You help me to fulfill them. They point out the way, but You give strength to walk in it.

They do all outwardly, but You instruct and enlighten the heart. They water only outwardly, but You give the inward growth. They cry aloud in words, but You give understanding to those who hear.

3. Therefore, do not let Moses speak to me, but only You, Lord Jesus, the eternal Truth; otherwise I may die and be fruitless, warmed outwardly, but not inflamed within. Then would I receive severe judgment, for I would have heard Your word and not obeyed it, known it and not loved it, believed it and not kept it.

Speak to me Yourself, *Lord, for Your servant is listening* (1 Sam 3:9). *You alone have the words of eternal life* (Jn 6:69); speak them to me that they may comfort my soul, and help me to amend my whole life: all to Your everlasting honor and glory.

CHAPTER 3

The Words of God Are to Be Heard with Humility; Many Fail to Reflect on Them

CHRIST: My child, hear My words and follow them; for they are most sweet and far exceed the learning and wisdom of the philosophers and all the wise of the world. My words are spirit and life, and not within the scope of human understanding.

They are not to be adapted or applied to the vain complacency of the hearer, but are to be heard in silence, with humility and reverence, with deep affection and in great tranquility of body and soul.

2. *Disciple: Blessed is the person You admonish, O Lord, the person You teach by means of Your law, giving respite in times of misfortune* (Ps 94:12-13), so that such a person may not be left desolate upon the earth.

3. *Christ:* Then our Lord answered: I have taught Prophets from the beginning and I continue to speak to all persons; but many have hardened their hearts and are deaf to My voice. Many prefer to listen to the world than to God, and to follow the desires of the flesh than the will of God.

The world promises things of short duration and little value; yet with what great eagerness is it served. I promise everlasting things of great value, but human hearts are indifferent and unmoved.

4. Who is there that serves and obeys Me with the devotion and obedience such a one gives

to the world and its rulers? *Blush for shame, says the sea!* (Isa 23:4). And why is this? For a small reward people will undertake long journeys, but for life everlasting they will scarcely lift their feet from the ground.

Often a thing of little worth is diligently sought after and sometimes they quarrel over a mere coin. Persons will toil day and night for a trifling advantage, or the mere promise of it.

5. For shame! For the good that never changes, for the reward no one can rightly value, for the highest honor and glory that will never end, people are unwilling to make the slightest effort.

Be ashamed, you slothful and complaining servant of God, that there are those who are more ready for the works of death than you are to win everlasting life; and that they enjoy the pursuit of vanities more than you do the pursuit of truth. Yet, they are often deceived in those things in which they hoped; but My promise deceives no one.

The person who trusts in Me is never sent away empty. What I have promised, I will do; and what I have said, I will fulfill, if only a person remains faithful in My love to the end. I am the rewarder of all good people and the mighty tester of all the devout.

6. Write My words carefully in your heart and often meditate on them; for they will be very necessary to you in the time of temptation. What you fail to understand when you read will be revealed to you at the time of My coming.

There are two ways in which I visit My elect: with temptation and with consolation. Also, there are two lessons which I daily read them: in one I rebuke their vices and in the other I stir them up to increase in virtue. Those who have heard My words and ignored them have One Who shall judge them on the last day.

A Prayer to Obtain the Grace of Devotion

7. *Disciple:* O Lord Jesus, You are all my good and the Source of all I have. What am I, Lord, that I should dare to speak to You? I am Your poorest servant, a miserable worm, poorer and more despicable than I can dare to say. Look at me, Lord, for I am nothing, I have nothing and I can do nothing of myself.

You alone are good, just, and holy and can do all things. You give all things, and You fill all things with Your goodness, leaving only the sinner empty and devoid of heavenly comfort. Remember Your mercies and fill my heart with Your grace, for You do not will that Your works become vain in me.

8. How can I bear the miseries of this life without Your grace and mercy to strengthen me? Do not turn Your face from me and do not delay to visit me with Your comfort; otherwise my soul will become *like a parched land* (Ps 143:6) to You without the water of grace.

Lord, *teach me to do Your will* (Ps 143:10) and to live worthily and humbly in Your sight. You are my wisdom and You know me as I truly am; You knew me before the world was made, and before I was born into this life.

CHAPTER 4

We Should Walk before God in Truth and Humility

CHRIST: My child, *walk before Me in truth* (1 Ki 2:4) and simplicity of heart—without pretense. Those who so walk will be shielded from the attacks of the evil one; and Truth shall free them from deceivers and the detractions of evil people.

If Truth makes you free, you will be free indeed and the vain words of human beings will not bother you.

Disciple: Lord, what You say is true; and I pray You to let it be done to me. Let Your truth teach me and guide me, and lead me at last to eternal salvation. Let it deliver me from all evil desires and inordinate love, that I may walk with You in liberty of heart.

2. *Christ:* I will teach you what is right and pleasing to Me. Think about your sins with great displeasure and deep sorrow in your heart, never considering yourself virtuous because of your good deeds. Rather, reflect on how great a sinner you are, subject to the many passions which envelop you.

Left to yourself, you revert to nothing, soon fall, soon are overcome, soon are disturbed and easily discouraged. There is nothing for which you can take credit, but much for which you ought to despise yourself; for you are far weaker in spiritual things than you realize.

3. Therefore, let nothing seem great to you, nothing valuable or remarkable, nothing worthy of your praise except what is eternal. Let the everlasting Truth be acceptable and regarded by you above all other things, and let your own sins and wretchedness grieve you.

Fear nothing so much, blame and avoid nothing so much as your sins and vices, which ought to distress you more than the loss of all worldly possessions. There are some who are not sincere in their conduct with Me, but, led by curiosity and pride to search the mysteries of God, neglect themselves and their spiritual welfare.

Such people often fall into grave temptations and sins because of their pride and curiosity. So I leave them to their own devices without My help and counsel.

4. Dread the judgments of God; tremble before the anger of the Almighty. Do not presume to search His secrets, but thoroughly search your own iniquities: how often and how grievously you have offended Him and how much good you might have done but neglected to do.

Some seek their devotion in books, others in pictures and still others in outward symbols and figures. Some have Me on their lips, but seldom in their hearts.

There are others whose reason has been enlightened and whose affections so purified from the love of worldly things that they long only for the eternal, and for whom it is a great burden to be subject to the necessities of the body. These understand well what the Spirit of Truth speaks in their souls.

He teaches them to have contempt for earthly things and to love those of heaven; to ignore the world and to long day and night for heaven.

CHAPTER 5

On the Wonderful Effect of the Love of God

D*ISCIPLE:* May You be blessed, O Heavenly Father, Father of my Lord, Jesus Christ, because You have consented to be mindful of me, poor sinner that I am. O Father of mercies and God of all comfort, I thank You, that sometimes You are pleased to console me with Your gracious presence, though I am unworthy of such consolation.

I bless You and glorify You always, together with Your Son and the Holy Spirit, the Comforter, forever and ever. O my Lord, God, most faithful Lover, when You come into my heart, my whole being is filled with joy. You are my glory and the joy of my heart; *my hope and refuge in the time of tribulation* (Ps 59:17).

2. You know how weak in love and imperfect in virtue I am and how much I stand in need of Your strength and comfort. Please, Lord, visit me often and instruct me in Your holy teachings.

Deliver me from evil passions and heal my heart from all disorderly affections, so that being healed inwardly and well purified, I may become ready to love You, strong to suffer for You, and firm to persevere.

3. Love is a strong force—a great good in every way; it alone can make our burdens light, and alone it bears in equal balance what is pleasing and displeasing. It carries a burden and does not feel it; it makes all that is bitter taste sweet.

The noble love of Jesus urges us to do great things and spurs us on to desire perfection. Love tends upward to God and is not occupied with the things of earth. Love also will be free from all worldly affections, so that its inner vision does not become dimmed, nor does it let itself be trapped by any temporal interest or downcast by misfortune.

Nothing is sweeter than love, nothing higher, nothing stronger, nothing larger, nothing more joyful, nothing fuller, nothing better in heaven or on earth; for love is born of God and can find its rest only in God above all He has created.

4. Such lovers fly high, run swiftly and rejoice. Their souls are free; they give all for all and have all in all. For they rest in One Supreme Goodness above all things, from Whom all other good flows and proceeds. They look not only at the gifts, but at the Giver, Who is above all gifts.

Love knows no limits, but is fervent above all measure. It feels no burden, makes light of labor, desiring to do more than it is able. Nothing is impossible to love, for it thinks that it can and may do all things for the Beloved.

Therefore it does and effects many things, while those who do not love falter and fail.

5. Love is ever watchful; it rests, but does not sleep; though weary, it is not tired; restricted, yet not hindered. Although it sees reason to fear, it is not dismayed; but like a spark of fire or a burning flame, it blazes upward to God by the fervor of its love, and through the help of His grace is delivered from all dangers.

Those who love thus know well what their voices mean when they cry out to God with all the ardor of their soul: You, Lord God, are my whole love and all my desire. You are all mine and I am all Yours.

6. Let my heart expand in Your love. Let me learn to know how sweet it is to serve You, how joyful it is to praise You, and to be dissolved in Your love. Oh, I am possessed by love and rise above myself because of the great fervor I feel through Your infinite goodness.

I will sing the canticle of love to You and will follow You, my Beloved, wherever You go, and may my soul never weary of praising You, rejoicing in Your love. I will love You more than myself and myself only for Your sake; I will love all others in You and for You, as Your law of love commands.

7. Love is swift, sincere, pious, joyful and glad; it is strong, patient, faithful, wise, forbearing, courageous, and is never self-seeking; for when people seek themselves, they cease to love.

Love is cautious, humble and upright; not weak, not flighty, nor concerned with trifles. It is sober, chaste, firm, quiet, and keeps guard over the senses.

Love is submissive and obedient to authority, mean and despicable in its own sight, devout and thankful to God. Love always trusts and hopes in God, even when it lacks fervor; for there is no living in love without some sorrow or pain.

8. Those who are not always ready to suffer and to stand disposed to the will of their Beloved are not worthy to be called lovers; for lovers must gladly embrace all hardship and bitter things for their Beloved, and never allow themselves to turn away from Him by adversity.

CHAPTER 6

On the Proof of a True Lover

CHRIST: My child, you are not yet a valiant and wise lover.

Disciple: Why, Lord?

Christ: Because with a little adversity you leave off what you have begun and eagerly seek outward consolation. Valiant lovers of God stand firm in time of temptation and pay no attention to the deceitful suggestions of their enemy, the devil. When all goes well with them, I please them; and so do I please them when things go wrong.

2. Wise lovers do not consider the gift of the Lover as much as they do the love of the Giver. They look more at the love than at the value of the gift; for their Beloved is far above His gifts.

PROOF OF TRUE LOVE—"A woman in the crowd called out to Him and said, 'Blessed is the womb that bore You. . . .' Jesus replied, 'Blessed, rather, are those who hear the word of God and obey it' " (Lk 11:27f).

Generous lovers are not content with the gift, but desire Me above any gift I can give them.

Therefore, do not be discouraged if sometimes you have less devotion toward Me or My Saints than you would wish. On the other hand, that good, spiritual desire you feel now and then toward your Lord is the gift of grace given to you for your comfort in this life and a foretaste of heavenly glory.

But it is not good to rely too much on such comforts that come and go, according to the will of the Giver. Strive always against temptations to sin and despise the suggestions of the devil, for this is a sign of virtue and of great merit.

3. Do not permit strange fantasies to disturb you, no matter what suggests them. Hold to your resolutions and keep your intention fixed on Me; nor think it is an illusion if sometimes you are rapt in ecstasy and then suddenly return to your usual levity of heart.

For these you endure unwillingly, and so long as you do not encourage them and they displease you, they will be cause of merit for you and not loss.

4. You know that our old enemy, the devil, uses every means he can to keep you from your good works and your prayer life—namely, from the worship you owe to Me and the veneration of the Saints, from meditating on My Passion, from the profitable reflection on your sins, from keeping watch over your heart and from a firm resolve to advance in virtue.

This fiend will suggest many idle and evil thoughts to draw you away from prayer and weary you with spiritual reading and other good works. A humble confession is obnoxious to him and, if he can, he will prevent you from receiving Holy Communion. Do not believe him, and pay no attention to him no matter how often he tries to trap you.

Turn his malice against him, saying to him: Begone, Satan, you wicked spirit, and be ashamed, for you are foul to suggest such things to me. Depart from me, you father of lies. You shall have no hold upon me; for Jesus Christ, my Savior, is with me as my valiant defender, and you shall be put to flight in utter confusion.

I would rather die in torment than give in to you. Be silent and cease your malice, for I will not listen to you no matter how much you tempt me. *The Lord is my light and my salvation; whom should I fear? Even if an army encamps against me, my heart will not succumb to fear. You are my help and my deliverer* (Pss 27:1, 3; 40:18).

5. Fight on like a good soldier; and if sometimes through weakness you fall, get up again and with greater strength than before, trust in My abundant grace. But be on your guard against self-complacency and pride; for it is through these that many are led into error, and sometimes into an almost incurable blindness of soul.

Let the downfall of those who foolishly rely on themselves be a warning to you and keep you always humble.

CHAPTER 7

How Grace Is to Be Kept Close through the Virtue of Humility

CHRIST: My child, it is better and safer for you to hide the grace of devotion. Do not speak much about it, nor think much of it; but rather belittle yourself more because of it, regarding yourself as unworthy of so gracious a gift from God.

Do not depend too much on such feelings of devotion which can quickly change into the opposite. When you have this great gift, think how wretched and poor you are without it. Progress in the spiritual life does not consist in having this grace of devotion, but rather in bearing the withdrawal and the absence of it humbly and patiently, without ceasing to pray or leaving your accustomed good works undone.

Do the best you can according to your ability; attend to your soul and do not be negligent in your duties because of dryness or any mental anxiety you may feel.

2. For there are many people who, when things do not go well for them, soon become impatient or lazy, and so set themselves back. Our life is not always ours to control; it is for God to dispose this as He wills: to give comfort when He wills, as much as He wills and to whom He wills, and no more.

Some imprudent people, through an indiscreet desire to have the grace of devotion, have damaged themselves, for they wished to do more than they were able. Not taking into account the limit of their gift or their own weakness, they chose to follow their inclinations rather than good judgment; and because they presumed to undertake more than was pleasing to God, they soon lost the grace they already had.

They were left poor and abandoned, for they thought they had built a nest in heaven for themselves. In this way they were taught not to rely on their own strength, but humbly to trust in God and His goodness.

Beginners and those inexperienced in the way of the Lord may easily fall into error and be deceived unless they seek the counsel of the wise.

3. But if they choose to follow their own judgment and refuse to be dissuaded from it, rather than take the advice of those with more experience, their end will be endangered. Seldom are the wise in their own estimation humble enough to allow others to guide them.

Therefore, it is better to have a little learning with humility than great learning with self-complacency. It is better to have a little learning with grace than much learning which fills you with pride.

Those persons are indiscreet who give themselves over to joy, forgetting their former desolation and the humble fear of God, which fears to lose the grace that was offered. They also are far from being virtuous, who, in time of trouble or adversity, give themselves up to despondency and do not place their confidence in Me as they ought.

4. They who feel too secure in time of peace become dejected and fearful in time of conflict and temptation. If only you could remain humble and little in your own opinion and keep the motions of your soul under control, you would not quickly fall into presumption or despair.

When you receive the gift of fervor, it is wise to consider how you will act when that fervor is withdrawn. Then when this happens, think that it may soon return to you, which, for My glory and your warning, I have withdrawn from you for a time.

5. When I put you to this test, it is more profitable for you than always to have things go according to your will. The merits of persons are not to be highly esteemed because such persons have many visions or spiritual consolations, or because they are well versed in Scripture, nor even by their being in a more elevated position.

But if they are firmly grounded in humility and filled with charity; if they seek purely the worship of God—looking upon themselves as nothing and sincerely despising themselves; and if they desire to be despised by others, then they may really hope that they have advanced spiritually and that in the end they will have the reward of God for all their labor.

CHAPTER 8

On the Lowly Esteem of Self in God's Sight

DISCIPLE: I will speak to You, Lord Jesus, *I who am but dust and ashes* (Gen 18:27). If I think myself any better, You stand opposed to me, and what is more, my own sins bear witness against me. This evidence I cannot deny.

But if I humble myself, admit my insignificance, rid myself of all self-esteem, and regard myself as the mere dust that I am, then Your grace will come to me and the light of Your understanding enter into my heart; so that, through perfect knowledge of my wretchedness, all self-esteem will be lost in the depth of my own nothingness.

There You show me what I truly am, what I have been, and what I have become; for I am nothing and I did not know it. Left to myself, I realize then that I am nothing and that all is weakness and imperfection.

But the moment You look upon me, I soon become strong and am filled with new joy. How wonderful it is that I am so quickly lifted up and so lovingly supported by You, I who of myself tend downward to earthly things.

2. Lord, Your love is the cause of this, which goes before me and helps me in all my necessities; it protects me from those grave dangers to which I am most prone to succumb. I have lost You and

myself, too, by my disordered self-love; by seeking You again, I found both You and myself.

From now on, therefore, I will make myself completely insignificant and more earnestly seek You; for You, Lord Jesus, deal with me far above what I deserve—indeed far above all that I dare to ask or hope for.

3. Blessed are You, O Lord, in all Your works, for though I am unworthy of any good, You continually surround me with Your kindness, which is extended even to those who are ungrateful to You or have turned away from You.

Lord, please turn us back to You again so that we may become grateful, humble and devout; for You are our help, our salvation and the strength of our body and soul.

CHAPTER 9

How All Things Are to Be Referred to God, Our Last End

CHRIST: My child, if you desire true happiness, then I must be the ultimate goal of all your works. Too often your affections are inclined toward yourself and other creatures; direct them toward Me, and they will be purified.

If you set yourself as the end of your work, you will soon lose heart and become dry. Refer all things to Me, for I have given all. Consider all things as flowing forth from My sovereign goodness, and return all things to Me, as to their source.

2. From Me, as from a living spring, both small and great, poor and rich, draw living water. They who serve Me freely and willingly will receive grace for grace; but they who glorify themselves, or take delight in anything else besides Me, will not be established in perfect joy, nor will their hearts be enlarged; but they will be frustrated and confined in many ways.

Therefore, do not think you are virtuous, nor attribute virtue to anyone, but give all credit to God, without Whom human beings have nothing. I have given all and I will have all referred back to Me, and I strictly require your gratitude for what I have given.

3. This is the truth by which all vainglory is driven away. If heavenly grace and true charity enter into your heart, there will be no room for envy, no narrowness of heart, nor will self-love rule in you. For the charity of God overcomes all and will expand and set on fire the powers of your soul.

If you understand rightly, you will rejoice only in Me, and in Me alone you will place your confidence; for *no one is good but God alone* (Lk 18:19), and He alone is to be honored above all things and in all things shall He be blessed.

CHAPTER 10

On the Joy of Serving God and Abandoning the World

DISCIPLE: I will speak to You again, O Lord, for I cannot be silent. I will say in Your hearing, my God and my King, Who is in heaven: *"How great is Your goodness, O Lord, which You have stored up for those who fear You"* (Ps 31:20). What then are You to those who love You and serve You with all their heart?

Truly, it is the indescribable sweetness of contemplation which You give to those who love You. In this You have shown the tenderness of Your charity, that when I had no being You made me; and when I strayed away from You, You brought me back again to serve You and commanded me to love You.

2. O Fountain of love eternal, what shall I say to You? How can I forget You, Who have condescended to remember me, even when I was on the verge of being lost because of my sins? You have shown me Your mercy beyond all my hope, and restored me to Your grace and friendship far beyond anything I deserved. What return can I make to You for so great a favor?

It is not granted to all persons to abandon the world and to lead a solitary life in Your service. Actually, it is no great thing for me to serve You, for every creature is bound to serve You. What really amazes me is that You admit into Your

JESUS TELLS US TO SERVE GOD AND SPURN SATAN—"Depart from My sight, Satan! . . . 'You shall worship the Lord your God; and Him alone shall you serve' " (Mt 4:10f).

service such an unworthy one as I, and make me one with Your chosen servants.

3. You know, O Lord, all that I have is Yours, even those things with which I serve You. But in Your goodness, it is rather You Who serve me than I You.

For the heavens and the earth, which You have created for our use, are ready day by day to carry out Your commands. You have also appointed Your Angels to serve our needs. And as if this were not enough, You stoop to serve us Yourself, promising to give Yourself to us.

4. And now what shall I give You in return for these innumerable blessings? O my God, if only I could serve You all the days of my life—or even for one day be able to serve You faithfully; for You are worthy of all honor, service and praise forever.

You are my Lord and my God, and I am Your poorest servant, bound to serve You with all my strength and never to grow weary of praising You. This is my desire, this I implore You: that I may always praise You and that You will supply whatever is wanting to me.

5. It is a great honor to serve You, and to despise all things for love of You. Those who freely give themselves to Your holy service will receive great grace.

They will find the comfort of the Holy Spirit with all its sweetness, who, for love of You, have renounced all carnal pleasures. They who, for Your Name's sake, enter upon the narrow way, laying aside all worldly business, will have great spiritual freedom.

6. O happy and joyful service of God, which makes us free and holy! O holy state of religion, which makes us like the Angels, pleasing to God, feared by evil spirits, and edifying to all the faithful.

Such service is worthy to be desired and embraced, which earns for us the greatest good and a joy that will never end.

CHAPTER 11

On the Need to Examine and Moderate the Desires of the Heart

C*HRIST:* My child, you still have many things to learn, which you have not yet learned well.

2. *Disciple:* What are these things, Lord?

3. *Christ:* That you conform your desires and affections to My good pleasure, that you be not full of self-love, but a zealous follower of My will in all things. I understand well how desires sway you this way or that; but you should consider whether you are moved mainly for My honor or for your own interests.

If I am the cause, you will be at peace whatever I do with you. But if self-interest is your motive, this will hinder you and drag you down.

4. Be careful, therefore, not to rely too much on your own desire without consulting Me, lest perhaps you regret it later on, or be dissatisfied

with what pleased you at first. Not every inclination which appears to be good and holy should be followed at once; on the other hand, neither is every undesirable inclination hastily to be rejected.

Sometimes it is well for people to restrain those inclinations and desires—good in themselves— lest through impulsiveness they become distracted in mind, or an obstacle to the spiritual progress of others; or again, through the opposition of others, become disturbed and fall.

5. There are times when we must use violence and courageously resist our sensual appetite, having no regard for the likes and dislikes of the flesh; but rather, making sure that the body, despite its protests, becomes subject to the spirit.

It must be chastised and compelled to serve, until it is ready to obey in all things what the soul commands, and until it learns to be content with little, to delight in simple things and not to complain at any inconvenience.

CHAPTER 12

On Acquiring Patience in the Struggle against Concupiscence

DISCIPLE: O my Lord, God, I can see that patience is very necessary for me, for this life is full of many disturbing things. No matter how I may plan my life so as to have peace, life cannot be without struggle and sorrow.

2. *Christ:* My child, certainly this is true. It is not My will that you look for peace without temptations or difficulties; on the contrary, you must believe that you have found peace when you have been tried by tribulations and adversity. If you say that you cannot stand much suffering, how will you endure the fires of purgatory?

Always choose the lesser of two evils. Therefore, try to bear the evils of this life patiently for the love of God, that you may escape greater pains in the world to come. Do you think that worldly persons suffer little or nothing? You will find this is not so, even among the most privileged.

3. But perhaps you will say that others have many pleasures and follow their own will so much that they count their adversities as small.

4. Certainly it is true that they have their own way now. But how long do you think that will last? For as smoke vanishes into thin air, so shall they who are rich in this world's goods, leaving not a trace of the pleasures they once enjoyed.

Even while they live, they are not without bitterness, distrust, and fear of losing those pleasures they possess; for these very things from which they derive their greatest enjoyment often repay them with unhappiness. And it is just that this is so; that inasmuch as they seek delight in inordinate pleasures, they should not find full satisfaction without confusion and bitterness.

Oh, how short, how false and inordinate are all the pleasures of this world! But because of their excesses and blindness, worldly people do not see this; but like dumb beasts, for a few temporary and corruptible pleasures in this life, they plunge headlong into everlasting death.

So, my child, *do not go after your concupiscence, but turn away from your own will* (Sir 18:30). *Delight in your God* and fix your will firmly in Him, *and He will give you what your heart desires* (Ps 37:4).

5. If you will have abundant consolation and the comfort that comes from God, you will be blessed if you hold all worldly things in contempt, cutting yourself off from all sordid gratification, and abundant consolation will be given to you.

The more you withdraw from creature comforts, the sweeter and more lasting will be the comfort you find in Me. But in the beginning you will not attain to these without struggle and labor; for your old habits will stand in your way, but better ones will overcome them.

The body will complain, but it will be overcome by fervor of spirit. Our ancient enemy, the devil, will tempt you and hinder you, if he can, but devout prayer will drive him away; and by useful employment, his way will be blocked and he will not dare to come near you.

CHAPTER 13

On Humble Obedience after the Example of Our Lord, Jesus Christ

CHRIST: My child, they who try to withdraw themselves from obedience withdraw themselves from grace. They who seek personal privileges lose those which are shared by all.

If people do not freely and willingly submit themselves to a superior, it is a sign that their flesh is not completely under their control, but that it often rebels and complains. Therefore, if you want to subdue your lower nature, first learn to obey your superior.

If the inner person is strong, the outward enemy is sooner overcome. There is no worse or more troublesome enemy to your soul than yourself, as long as your flesh is not under the control of your will.

Therefore, it is an absolute necessity for you to acquire a true contempt of yourself, if you would prevail over flesh and blood. But because you still love yourself in the wrong way, you are afraid to resign your will entirely to the will of another.

2. But is it such a great thing for you, who are but dust and nothingness, to submit yourself to a man for My sake, when I, the Almighty and Most High God, Creator of all things, humbly submitted Myself to human beings for your sake? I became the lowliest and the least of human beings, so that you might overcome your pride through My humility.

You who are but ashes, learn to obey; you who are but the dust of the earth, learn to humble yourself and to bow beneath the feet of others for My sake. Learn to break your own will and to give yourself to all subjection.

3. Direct your wrath against yourself, and do not allow pride to rule over you; but show yourself to be so submissive, so insignificant, that all may walk over you and trample you underfoot like the mud in the streets.

What have you to complain of, vain person? O wretched sinner that you are, what answer can you justly make to those who rebuke you, since you have so often offended God and so often deserved the punishment of hell?

In spite of all this, My merciful eye has spared you, for your soul is precious in My sight; so that you might know My great love for you, and be ever grateful to Me in return, and give yourself to perfect and true humility, and suffer the contempt of others for My sake.

CHAPTER 14

On Considering the Secret Judgments of God So That We Do Not Become Proud of Our Good Works

DISCIPLE: O Lord, Your judgments sound forth like peals of thunder over my head and all my bones shake and tremble with fear, and my soul is seized with trembling. I am astounded when I consider that even the heavens are not pure in Your sight. You found sin among the Angels and did not spare them; what then will become of me?

Stars fell from heaven (Rev 6:13); what hope can I have, who am but dust? Some whose works seemed worthy of praise have fallen to the depths, and those who were fed with the Bread of Angels I have seen delighted with the husks of swine, that is, in pleasures of the flesh.

2. There can be no hope of holiness, O Lord, if You withdraw Your merciful hand. No wisdom can benefit us, if You cease to rule; nor strength be any support, if You do not preserve us. No chastity is secure, if You do not defend it; no self-protection can avail us, if You do not keep watch over us; for if You abandon us, we sink and are lost.

But when You visit us with Your grace, we are lifted up and restored to life. We have no stability, but we are made firm by You; we are cold, but You stir us to fervor of spirit.

3. Oh, what a lowly and humble opinion I ought to have of myself, and how little I ought to regard whatever good I may seem to have! How deeply I ought to submit myself to Your profound judgments, where I find myself to be nothing else but nothing—altogether nothing!

O Substance, immense beyond all weight! O Sea to whose furthest shore no one can ever sail, where I find my substance to be nothing, absolutely nothing! Where is there any hiding place for pride, and where is the confidence I had in my supposed virtue? All self-esteem is swallowed up in the depths of Your hidden judgments upon me.

4. What is all flesh in Your sight? Shall clay glorify itself against its Maker? How can any persons deceive themselves with empty praises whose hearts are subject to truth in God?

All the world cannot move them to pride whom Truth has made subject to Himself; nor may they whose whole trust rests in God be deceived by flattering tongues. They see well that all who speak are nothing, for they shall fade away with the sound of their words, *but the truth of the Lord endures forever* (Ps 116:2).

CHAPTER 15

On How We Are to Conduct Ourselves in Our Desires

CHRIST: My child, in every circumstance this is how you should pray: "Lord, if it be Your will, so let it be, and if it be to Your honor, let it be fulfilled in Your Name. Lord, if this be for my good, give me the grace to use it for Your honor; but if You know that it will be harmful to me and not profitable for the good of my soul, then take away from me such a desire."

Not every desire comes from the Holy Spirit, even though it seems good to you. It is difficult to judge rightly whether a good or evil spirit urges you to desire this or that, or whether you are prompted by your own spirit. Many have been deceived in the end who at first thought they were guided by the Holy Spirit.

2. Therefore, it is with fear of God and a humble heart that you should desire and ask for whatever comes to your mind as desirable. With entire abandonment of yourself to God, commit all things to Me, saying: "Lord, You know what is best for me; let it be done according to Your will. Give me what You will, in whatever measure You will and at whatever time You will.

"Do with me what You know to be best, as pleases You best and as will best promote Your glory. Put me where You will and freely do with me in all things according to Your will.

"Am I not Your creature, and in Your hands, for You lead me about and turn me about as You will? I am Your servant, ready to do all things at Your command; for I do not want to live for myself, but only for You. If only I could do this worthily and perfectly!"

A Prayer for Fulfilling the Will of God

3. O most merciful Jesus, grant me Your grace, that it may remain with me always and persevere with me to the end. Grant me always to will and desire what is most pleasing and acceptable to You.

Let Your will be mine, and let my will always follow Yours in perfect conformity with it. Let my will and desires always be one with Yours; and let me be unable to will or not to will except as You will or do not will.

4. Grant that I may die to all worldly things, and that I may be despised and unknown for love

COMPLETE TRUST IN JESUS—"The centurion replied [to Jesus], 'Lord, I am not worthy to have You come under my roof. But simply say the word and my servant will be healed. . . .' Jesus said to the centurion, 'Return home. Your petition has been granted because of your faith' " (Mt 8:8, 13).

of You. Grant, above all things to be desired, that I may find rest in You, and that in Your heart alone may be my peace. You, O Lord, give true peace to the heart and perfect rest to body and soul.

Apart from You, all is difficult and never still. In that peace, in You Who are the one, supreme and eternal Good, *I will sleep and take my rest* (Ps 4:9). Amen.

CHAPTER 16

True Solace Is to Be Sought in God Alone

DISCIPLE: Whatever I can desire or imagine for my comfort, I do not expect here but hereafter. If I alone should have all the comforts of this world and could enjoy all its pleasures according to my own desire and without sin, it is certain that they could not last long.

Therefore my soul can never be fully comforted, nor be perfectly refreshed except in God, the comforter of the poor in spirit and the refuge of the humble.

Wait a little while, my soul, await the promise of God, and you will have the fullness of all that is good in heaven. If you yearn inordinately for the good things of this life, you will lose those which are heavenly and eternal.

Use temporal things properly, but always desire what is eternal. Temporal things can never fully satisfy you, for you were not created to enjoy them alone.

2. Even though you possessed all temporal goods, they could not make you happy and blessed; for your blessedness and happiness lie only in God, Who has made all things from nothing. Your true happiness is not such as is praised by the foolish lovers of the world, but such as good and faithful followers of Christ look forward to in the kingdom of heaven. The spiritual and pure of heart, whose conversation is in heaven, sometimes have a foretaste of such happiness in this present life.

All worldly solace and all human comfort is empty and short-lived; but blessed is that comfort which is inwardly received from the Truth.

3. Devout persons always carry Jesus, their Consoler, with them, and say to Him: Be with me, Lord Jesus, in every place and at all times, that I may have the special grace to forgo all human solace for love of You; and if Your comfort is withdrawn, let Your will and Your just trial of me be like the greatest comfort. For *He will not always rebuke, nor will He remain angry forever* (Ps 103:9).

CHAPTER 17

That All Our Cares Must Be Placed in God

CHRIST: My child, permit Me to do with you what I will, for I know what is best for you. You think as a human being and judge things according to human reason; but you are often swayed by your feelings and worldly attitudes, so that you can easily be deceived and make mistakes.

Disciple: Lord, everything You say is true. Your providence is far better for me than any care I can take of myself. Those who do not put all their trust in You run a great risk of falling. Therefore, Lord, if only my will remain firmly fixed in You, do with me as You please, for whatever You do with me can only be good.

2. If it is Your will that I be in light, may You be blessed, Lord; but if it is Your will that I be in darkness, may You also be blessed. If, in Your mercy, You comfort me, be You blessed; but if it is Your will that I be afflicted, still be You always blessed.

3. *Christ:* My child, this is how you must stand if you want to walk beside Me: you must be as ready to suffer as to rejoice, as willing to be needy and poor as to be rich and have abundance.

4. *Disciple:* Lord, I willingly bear for You whatever You are pleased to give me. With indifference I will take from Your hand good and bad, bitter and sweet, joy and sorrow; and for all these things that may happen to me, I thank You with all my heart.

Keep me from sin, Lord, and I will fear neither death nor hell. Do not blot my name out of the book of life, and then whatever trouble befalls me will not disturb me.

CHAPTER 18

That All Temporal Sorrows Are to Be Borne Patiently after the Example of Christ

C*HRIST:* My child, I came down from heaven to save you; I took upon Myself your miseries, not because I had to do so, but out of love. I wanted you to learn patience and to bear the trials of this life without complaint, as I have done for you.

From the hour of My birth until My death upon the cross, I was never without sorrow or suffering. I endured the want of temporal things; many and frequent were the complaints I heard against Me; I humbly bore shame and insults. I received ingratitude for My benefits, blasphemies for My miracles, and rebukes for My true doctrine.

2. *Disciple:* Lord, since You were patient during Your lifetime, thereby fulfilling the will of Your Father, it is only right that I, a most wretched sinner, should bear all things patiently according to Your will and, for as long as it pleases You, should support the burden of this corruptible life for the sake of my soul's salvation.

This life is tedious and a burden to the soul, but now through Your grace it has become very meritorious; and by Your own example and that of Your holy Saints, it has been made easier and more hopeful for the weak. The present is also much richer in consolation than it was under the Old Law, when the gate of heaven was shut and the way to it obscure and so few desired to seek it.

Even the just of those days, who were ordained to be saved, could not enter the kingdom of heaven before You paid their debt by Your sacred Passion and Death.

3. Oh, what gratitude am I not bound to return to You for Your great mercy in showing me, and all the faithful who will follow You, the true and straight way to Your kingdom! Your holy life is our way; and by holy patience we make our way to You, Who are our head.

Had You not gone before and shown us the way, who would have even tried to follow You? How many would have lagged behind had they not Your blessed example before their eyes! We are still slow and lukewarm, though we have heard of all Your miracles and Your doctrine; what would we be if we had not Your life to guide us? Certainly our minds and desires would have been attached to worldly things.

CHAPTER 19

On the Patient Suffering of Injuries, And Who Is Really Patient

CHRIST: What are you saying, My child? Stop complaining and consider My Passion and the sufferings of My Saints. *You have not yet resisted to the point of shedding your blood* (Heb 12:4). What you suffer is but little compared with those who have borne so much for Me, who have been strongly tempted, grievously afflicted and put to the test in so many ways. You ought to remind yourself of the intense sufferings that others have endured for Me, that you may bear your own little miseries more easily.

If they do not seem so little to you, take care that you do not magnify them because of your impatience. However, whether they are little or great, always try to bear them patiently, willingly, and without complaint.

2. The better disposed you are to suffer them, the more wisely you act and the more merit you will have, because you have prepared yourself for it and are well disposed to accept it.

Do not ever say: "I cannot endure this thing from such a person, nor should this be expected of me, for that person has done me a great wrong, accusing me of things I never thought of; but from someone else, I am willing to put up with what I think is fitting for me to suffer." This is a foolish thought, for you are forgetting the virtue of patience and by Whom its practice is rewarded, only considering the persons and the offenses done.

3. Therefore, they are not truly patient who will suffer only as much as they please and from whom they please. Persons who are really patient do not mind who causes their suffering—whether it be their superior, an equal, or someone of lower rank, or whether such a person is good and holy, or evil and unworthy.

But whenever any adversity happens to them, whatever it is and from whomever it comes, or how often, they accept all gratefully as from the hand of God and consider it as a great benefit; for they well know that there is nothing we can suffer for God that goes without merit.

4. So, be ready to fight to win the victory. Without a conflict you cannot obtain the crown of patience. If you reject the suffering, you reject the crown also; but if you wish to be crowned, resist strongly and suffer patiently. There is no rest without labor, nor victory without battle.

5. *Disciple:* O Lord Jesus, make possible to me by grace what is impossible by nature. You know well how little I can bear and how easily I am upset by a little adversity.

Therefore, I beseech You, that hereafter any trouble or adversity may be loved and desired by me for Your Name, for it is very good and profitable to my soul to suffer and be afflicted for You.

CHAPTER 20

On Acknowledging Our Own Infirmities and the Miseries of This Life

D*ISCIPLE:* Lord, I will acknowledge my sin before You and confess my instability. Often some trivial thing depresses me, leaving me dull and slow to do good works. I resolve to stand firm; but at the slightest temptation, I am set back.

Sometimes from a mere trifle a grievous temptation arises; and just when I feel sure and think I have the upper hand, suddenly I am almost overcome by the least thing.

2. Therefore, dear Lord, see my wretchedness and my frailty, which are best known to You above all others. Have compassion on me and deliver me from sinking into the mire of sin, that I may not stick fast in it. But this is what disturbs me and often confounds me in Your sight, that I am so prone to fall and so weak in resisting my passions.

And though I do not give in to them altogether, yet their assaults are troublesome to me, so that I am wearied by the daily conflict. Yet I know such conflict is not at all unprofitable to me; for by this I see my infirmities better and understand that such evil fantasies rush in upon me more easily than they depart.

3. Would that You, most powerful God of Israel, the lover of all faithful souls, would look upon the sorrow and struggle of Your poorest servant, and come to my assistance in all that I must do. Strengthen me, O Lord, with heavenly fortitude, so that the old enemy, the devil and my wretched flesh—not yet fully subject to the spirit—may not prevail over me; for it is against them that I must fight continually during this wretched life.

And what kind of life this is, where troubles and miseries are never wanting and everywhere there lurk snares and enemies! For as soon as one temptation or trouble goes away, another comes; and while the first struggle is still on, many others suddenly rise up unexpectedly.

4. How, then, can this life be loved, which is so full of bitterness and subject to so many trials? How can it even be called life since it brings forth so many deaths and spiritual plagues? Yet it is loved and many seek all their pleasure in it.

The world is often blamed for being deceitful and vain, yet it is not easily given up, especially when the desires of the flesh take hold. Some things lead us to love the world, others to despise it.

Those things that lead a person to love the world are *sensual desires, the enticements that lure the eyes, the pride in riches* (1 Jn 2:16); but the pains and miseries that follow them breed a hatred of and disgust with the world.

5. But, sad to say, a little pleasure dominates the minds of the worldly, driving out of their hearts all heavenly desires, to such an extent that many imagine that joy is to be found in living under such sensual pleasures. That is because they have neither seen nor tasted the sweetness of God and the inward joy of virtue.

But those who utterly despise the world and strive to live under holy discipline experience the heavenly sweetness promised to spiritual persons; they also see the errors of the world and how it is deceived in so many ways.

CHAPTER 21

On How We Are to Rest in God above All Things

D*ISCIPLE:* Above all things and in all things rest, my soul, in the Lord, your God, for He is the eternal rest of the Angels and Saints. O most loving Jesus, give me this special grace to rest in You above all created things; above all health and beauty, above all glory and honor, above all dignity and power, above all knowledge and prudence, above all riches and talents, above all joy and gladness, above all fame and praise, above all sweetness and consolation, above all hope and promise, above all merit and desire, above all gifts and rewards that You may give or send—except Yourself—above all joy or happiness that the human mind and heart can grasp or feel; above Angels and Archangels, above all the heavenly hosts as well; above all things visible and invisible, and above all that is not You, my God.

2. For You alone, O Lord God, are the greatest good; You alone are most high and most mighty; You alone are most sufficient and perfect; You alone are most sweet and consoling. You alone are most fair and loving, You alone are most noble and most glorious above all things. In You all good things are found existing in all their perfection, and have always been, and always shall be.

Therefore, anything You give me besides Yourself, anything You reveal or promise me concerning Yourself, is all too little and insufficient for me; because my heart cannot rest nor fully be content until it rises above all Your gifts and all You have created, and rests in You.

3. O Jesus Christ, most loving Spouse, most pure Lover, Ruler of all creation, who will give me wings of perfect freedom to fly to You and in You to repose? When shall I be fully granted the perfect liberty to see how sweet You are, O Lord, my God? When shall I be so perfectly recollected in You as not to be aware of myself, but only You, above all the things of sense, in a way not known to all?

But now how often I sigh and complain of the miseries of this life. I daily meet with many evils in this vale of miseries, which often trouble me, sadden me and darken my way; they often hinder and distract me, lure and ensnare me, preventing me from going freely to You, from enjoying the sweet embrace always granted to Your blessed spirits. Let my sighs and many desolations move Your heart and incline You to hear me.

4. O Jesus, light and brightness of eternal glory, the joy and consolation of all Christians who labor as pilgrims in this sinful world, no words can express the desires of my heart; but let my very silence speak to You and say: How long, O Lord, will You delay Your coming?

I trust that You will come soon to Your poor servant, make me joyful and deliver me from all my troubles. Come to me, dear Lord, for no day or hour is happy without You.

You are all joy and gladness, and without You all is barren and empty. I am miserable and, in a sense, a prisoner in chains until You visit me with the light of Your presence, give me liberty of spirit and turn Your friendly face toward me.

5. Others may seek whatever they please, but there is nothing that pleases me—nor ever shall— but You, my God, my hope and my eternal salvation. I will not remain silent nor cease to pray until Your grace returns to me and I hear You speak to my soul once more.

6. *Christ: Behold, I am here!* (Isa 58:9). *I come to you, for you have called Me* (1 Sam 3:9). Your tears and the longing of your heart, your humility and contrition, have moved Me to answer your prayer.

7. *Disciple:* Lord, I called You, for I long for Your presence and I am prepared to renounce all things for Your sake. It was You Who first moved me to seek You. Be You blessed, O Lord, for showing such goodness to me out of the abundance of Your mercy.

What more, O Lord, can I say in Your presence? I can only humble myself before You, ever mindful of my own iniquities. There is none like to You, O Lord, in heaven or on earth.

Your works are good, Your judgments are wise and true, and Your Providence governs all things. Praise and glory be to You, O Wisdom of the Father! Let my tongue, my soul, and all created things praise and bless You.

CHAPTER 22

On Remembering the Manifold Benefits of God

DISCIPLE: O Lord, open my heart to Your law and teach me to walk in the way of Your commandments. Give me the grace to understand Your will, and with great reverence and careful consideration remember all Your blessings, in general and in particular, so that from now on I may be able to thank You for them worthily.

But I know and confess that I am unable to praise and thank You adequately, not even for Your least gift; for indeed I am less than all the blessing You have given me. When I consider Your infinite nobility and worthiness, my spirit trembles before their greatness.

2. Lord, all that we have both in soul and body, whatever we possess within or without, naturally or supernaturally, comes from You and shows forth Your bountiful goodness, from Whom we have received everything that is good. Although one has received more and another less, yet all comes from You, and without You not even the least can be had.

Persons who have received more cannot boast as though they had gained it by their own merit, nor consider themselves above others, nor look down on those who have received less; for those are greater and more acceptable to You who attribute less to themselves, returning humble and devout thanks to You. Those who, through humility, consider themselves the least and most unworthy of all are fit to receive still greater blessings.

3. But persons who have received fewer gifts should not be sad nor envious of those who have been more enriched. Instead, they should look up to You and highly praise Your goodness because You bestow Your gifts generously, freely and willingly, without respect of persons.

All things come from You, and therefore in all things You should be praised. You know what is best suited to each person and why one has less and another more, and it is not our place to judge, but for You alone, by Whom the merits of each person are determined.

4. Lord, I count it as a benefit not to have those gifts which others can see and for which I might be complimented and praised. Furthermore, although persons should consider their own poverty and worthlessness, they should not be grieved or depressed, but rather they should feel happy and consoled; for You daily choose the humble and those who are despised by the world to be Your special friends and servants.

We have only to think of Your Apostles, whom You made princes of the whole world; yet they lived in this world without complaining—simple and unassuming—without malice or deceit, *and were even glad to suffer reproaches for Your Name* (Acts 5:41), so that what the world hated and rejected, they ardently embraced.

5. Nothing, therefore, should give greater joy to those who love You and have received Your

gifts than the accomplishment of Your will in them, according to Your eternal purpose. On this account they ought to be so contented and comforted that they would as soon be the least as others would desire to be the greatest.

They should enjoy as much peace in the lowest place as in the highest, be as glad to be despised and abject and of no name or reputation as to be preferred and greatly respected above others. Your will, Lord, and the honor of Your Name should come before all else and comfort and please them more than all the benefits that could be given them.

CHAPTER 23

On Four Things Which Bring Great Peace

C*HRIST:* My child, now I shall teach you the way of true peace and perfect liberty.

2. *Disciple:* Dear Lord, do as You say, for it will be a joy for me to hear this.

3. *Christ:* Try, my child, to do the will of another rather than your own. Always choose to have fewer riches rather than more. Always seek the lowest place and desire to be subject to all. Always wish for and pray that the will of God be accomplished in you. Such a person enters into the abode of true peace and inward rest.

4. *Disciple:* Lord, these four points which You have taught me contain great perfection. They are few in words, but full of meaning and abounding in virtue. If I could keep them faith-

fully, I would not be so easily upset. For as often as I feel restless and discontented, I find that I have departed from this sound doctrine.

But do You, Lord Jesus, Who can do all things and love to see the progress of the soul, increase Your grace in me to enable me to fulfill these words and accomplish my salvation.

A Prayer Against Evil Thoughts

5. *Disciple:* My Lord Jesus, I beseech You *not to go far from me, but come quickly and help me, my God* (Ps 71:12); for evil thoughts and worldly fears have risen up against me to harass my soul. How shall I break them down? How shall I pass through unharmed?

6. *Christ: I will go before you and humble the great ones of the earth* (Isa 45:2). I will open the gates of the prison and reveal My hidden secrets to you.

7. *Disciple:* Please, Lord, do as You say, and then these wicked thoughts shall flee from me. My one hope and consolation is to fly to You in every trouble, placing all my confidence in You and, calling to You from the depths of my heart, patiently to await Your consolation.

A Prayer for the Enlightening of Our Minds

8. *Disciple:* Enlighten me, Lord Jesus, with the brightness of internal light and dispel all darkness from my heart. Restrain my wayward thoughts and destroy all violent temptations which attack me.

Fight strongly for me and drive away the evil beasts—those enticing desires of the flesh—so that peace may rule by Your power and Your Name be praised abundantly in the temple of my soul, which is a clean and pure conscience.

Command the winds and storms of pride to cease; say to the sea of worldly desires: Be still; and to the north wind—the devil's temptation—Do not blow. Then there will be peace and tranquility.

9. *Send forth Your light and Your truth* (Ps 43:3) to shine upon the earth; for I am like the barren and dry earth until You enlighten me. Pour forth Your grace from above and water my heart with Your heavenly dew; let streams of devotion water the face of the earth; that it may bring forth good and perfect fruit.

Life up my mind so oppressed by the burden of sin and raise up my desire to heavenly things, so that having tasted the sweetness of supernatural joy, I may have no pleasure in the thought of earthly things.

10. Snatch me away and deliver me from the passing comfort of creatures; for nothing created can fully satisfy me. Unite me to Yourself with an inseparable bond of love, for You alone can satisfy the soul that loves You, and without You all else is worthless.

CHAPTER 24

On Avoiding Curious Inquiry into the Lives of Others

CHRIST: My child, do not be curious nor concern yourself with useless cares. *What is this or that to you? Do you follow Me* (Jn 21:22). What difference does it make to you whether this person is good or bad, or whether that one acts or speaks this way or that?

You do not have to answer for others, but you must give an account of yourself; so why do you interfere where it does not concern you? I know everyone and know all that is done under the sun; and I know how things stand with all persons—what they think, what they will and to what end their work is directed. All things are open to Me and all things are to be referred to Me.

So be at peace and do not let your mind be disturbed, and let those who want to pry into another's life be as busy as they will. In the long run, whatever they say and do will come back upon them, for they cannot deceive Me.

2. Do not be anxious to win a great name for yourself, to have the familiar acquaintance of many, nor the particular affection of any person; for such things cause distractions and will rob you of your peace of mind.

If only you would watch faithfully for My coming and open the door of your heart to Me, I would gladly speak to you and reveal to you My secrets. Be prudent, watchful in prayer, and humble yourself in all things.

CHAPTER 25

In What Consists Firm Peace of Heart and True Progress

CHRIST: My child, I have said: *"Peace I leave with you, My peace I give to you. Not as the world gives do I give it to you"* (Jn 14:27). All human beings desire peace; but not all will do what is necessary to obtain it. My peace is found among the humble and gentle of heart; you will find your peace by being patient. If you will listen to Me and follow My words, you will enjoy great peace.

2. *Disciple:* What, then, shall I do, Lord?

3. *Christ:* At all times pay attention to what you are doing and what you are saying, and make it your constant intention to please Me alone, neither desiring nor seeking anything apart from Me. Do not make rash judgments on what others say or do, and do not concern yourself about things not committed to your care.

If you follow this advice, you will be little or seldom disturbed. But never to feel any disturbance at all, nor to suffer any anguish of heart or bodily pain, is not the state of this present life, but of the life to come.

Do not think, therefore, that you have found true peace if you feel no grief, nor that all is well if no one opposes you; nor that you have arrived at perfection if everything goes the way you want it. Do not entertain any notion that you are a privileged person, particularly beloved by God, because you experience great fervor and devotion.

It is not in such things that a true lover of virtue is known, nor does a person's spiritual perfection and progress consist in these things.

4. *Disciple:* In what, then, Lord, does it consist?

5. *Christ:* In surrendering yourself with your whole heart to the will of God, and in not seeking yourself either in great things or small, in time or in eternity. If you remain constant in this attitude, you will continue to thank God whether things go well or otherwise, weighing all things in the one equal balance of His love.

And if you come to the state that, when inward consolation is withdrawn, you can move your heart to suffer still more, if God so wills—not considering it an injustice for you to suffer such great things, but acknowledging the justice of all My decisions—and still praise My holy Name, then you walk in the true way of peace and may hope without doubt to see Me face to face in everlasting joy in the kingdom of heaven.

And if you can arrive at a complete contempt of yourself, you can be sure of an abundance of peace, as much as is possible, during your earthly exile.

JESUS CONFORMS TO GOD'S WILL—"When the days for their purification were completed according to the law of Moses, they brought [Jesus] up to Jerusalem to present Him to the Lord" (Lk 2:22).

CHAPTER 26

On the Excellence of a Free Mind, the Reward of Humble Prayer Rather Than of Reading

DISCIPLE: Lord, it is the work of perfect persons never to let their minds slacken from the consideration of heavenly things, and to carry on amid many cares as though they had no care—not like an idle person, but by the special prerogative of a free mind, which clings to no creature by inordinate affection.

2. O most merciful God, I implore You to keep me from the cares of this world, so that I do not become overinvolved with them. Deliver me from the many demands of the body, lest I be ensnared by pleasure. Preserve me also from all hindrance of the soul that I may not be disheartened by my troubles and become downcast.

I do not ask to be kept from those vanities which the worldly covet so eagerly; but from those miseries—shared as a common burden by all humanity—which weigh so heavily upon the souls of Your servants and prevent them from entering into liberty of spirit as often as they would.

3. O my God, Who are sweetness unspeakable, turn into bitterness for me all carnal pleasures, which would lure me from the love of eternal things and urge me to take delight in some passing sensible good.

Do not let flesh and blood prevail over me, my God, nor let me be overcome by the world and its brief deceitful glory. Let not the devil, with all his cunning, ensnare me. Grant me the courage to resist, the patience to endure and the steadfastness to persevere.

Instead of worldly comfort, give me the sweet anointing of Your Holy Spirit, and in place of carnal love, fill my heart with the love of Your Holy Name.

4. Having to make use of food, drink, clothing and other necessities of the body is burdensome to a fervent soul. Grant me the grace to use such bodily necessities moderately and not to have an excessive desire for them.

We are not permitted to dispense with them altogether, for nature must be sustained, but Your holy law forbids unnecessary luxuries to be sought for our mere pleasure; otherwise the flesh would rebel against the spirit. I beseech You, Lord, that Your hand govern and direct me in all these matters so that I avoid excess.

CHAPTER 27

Nothing Withholds Us from God As Much As Self-Love

CHRIST: My child, you must give all for all, and keep nothing for your own. You know that self-love is more harmful to you than anything else. The inclination and attachment you have for a thing determines the hold it has on your heart. If your love is pure, simple and moderate, you will not be the slave of any earthly creature.

Do not desire that which you may not have, nor seek to possess anything which will impede your spiritual progress and deprive you of interior freedom. It is strange that you will not commit yourself to Me with all your heart, with all you can desire or possess.

2. Why do you languish in useless grief, or why are you so worn with needless cares? Resign yourself to My will and you will suffer no loss.

If you look for this thing or that, or wish to be in this place or that, simply for your own advantage or pleasure, you will never be at rest, nor free from anxiety. You will find something to dislike in everything, and there will be someone who will cross you no matter where you are.

3. Obtaining or increasing external possessions will not help you, but despising them and completely uprooting them from your heart will benefit you. Understand that this applies not only to money and worldly goods, but also to the pursuit of honor and the desire for vain praise.

All these things pass away with the world. The place helps little if the spirit of fervor is absent; and the peace you seek from without will not last long if you lack true inward peace.

You may change your place, but it will not improve you unless you stand firm and steadfast in Me. For when the occasion arises and you accept it, you will find what you were trying to avoid, and even more.

A Prayer for a Clean Heart and Heavenly Wisdom

4. *Disciple:* Strengthen me, O God, by the grace ofYour Holy Spirit. Grant me the power to grow in holiness and to empty my heart of all useless care and anxiety, that I may not be led by the desire for earthly things, whether of little or great value.

Help me to regard all things in this world as they are—passing and short-lived—realizing that I, too, will pass away with them. Nothing under the sun is lasting, but *all is vanity and a chase after wind* (Eccl 1:14). It is a wise person who understands this.

5. Give me Your heavenly wisdom, O Lord, that I may learn that the most important thing is to seek You and to find You and, above all things else, to love You. Help me to understand all other things as they truly are, according to Your wisdom.

Grant me the prudence to avoid all flatterers and to be patient with those who contradict me. It is great wisdom not to be influenced by garrulous speech, nor listen to soothing, tempting voices. By following such a road we will advance securely in the way we have begun.

CHAPTER 28

Against Slanderous Tongues

CHRIST: Do not take it seriously, my child, if people think evil of you and say things about you that you do not want to hear. You ought to have a worse opinion of yourself and to think that no one is weaker than you are.

If you are well recollected within, you will take no notice of fleeting words from without. It is a sign of wisdom, when evil words are spoken, to keep silence and to turn your heart to Me, refusing to be disturbed by man's judgment.

2. Do not let your peace of mind depend on what people say about you. You are still what you are, no matter whether they put a good or bad interpretation on your actions. Where will you find true peace and true glory if not in Me?

Certainly this is so. The person who neither aspires to please others nor fears to displease them will enjoy much peace; for all disquiet of heart and distraction of the senses come from disorderly affections and groundless fear.

CHAPTER 29

How We Should Call Upon God and Bless Him in Time of Tribulation

D*ISCIPLE:* Lord, may Your holy Name be blessed forever, for You have willed to send me this temptation and tribulation. I cannot escape it, and so I must fly to You for protection. You alone can help me and turn all to my good.

Lord, even now I am in trouble and my heart is uneasy, for I am harassed by my present affliction. And now, my beloved Father, what shall I say? I am caught in anguish on every side. *Save me from this hour? But it was for this that I came to this hour* (Jn 12:27), that You might be glorified when I am properly humbled and delivered by You.

Please, dear Lord, deliver me, for what can I do and where shall I go without You, wretched sinner that I am? Lord, give me patience this time too. Help me, O my God, and I will not fear or dread whatever trouble befalls me.

2. What shall I say now, Lord, in the midst of my distress? May Your will be done, for I well deserve to be afflicted and oppressed. I must bear it—and with patience—until the storm has passed and things grow better.

Your almighty hand is able to remove this temptation and to moderate its violence, as You have often done for me before, so that I do not give in to it, most merciful God! The harder this seems to me, the easier it is for You to bring about my deliverance; for this is *the change of the right hand of the Almighty* (Ps 77:11), to Whom be everlasting honor and glory.

CHAPTER 30

On Asking the Divine Assistance and on Confidence of Recovering Grace

CHRIST: My child, I am *the Lord, Who give strength on the day of distress* (Nah 1:7). Come to Me when all is not well with you. What hinders you most of all from receiving heavenly consolation is your slowness in turning to Me in prayer. Before you pray earnestly to Me, you first seek other comforts, trying to find distraction in outward things.

Hence it is that all these things are of little benefit to you until you realize that I alone am the One Who delivers those who trust in Me. There is no effectual help nor worthwhile counsel nor lasting remedy.

But now, having recovered your breath after the storm, gather your strength again in the light of My mercies, for I am near you to restore all, not only to their former state, but even to increase them abundantly and beyond measure.

2. *Is anything impossible for Me?* (Jer 32:27). Am I like human beings who promise something and do not live up to it? Where is your faith? Stand firm and persevere. Have courage and wait patiently; comfort will come to you when you most need it. Wait for Me, wait; and I will come soon to help you.

It is but a temptation that distresses you and a foolish fear that frightens you. This anxiety about future events brings you nothing but grief and more grief. *Today has troubles enough of its own* (Mt 6:34). It is a useless waste of time to worry or be elated about future events, which perhaps may never happen.

3. But it is part of human nature to be deluded by the images of imagination, and the sign of a soul that is still weak that you so easily follow the suggestions of your enemy, the devil, who does not care whether his deceits are true or false, or

whether he trips you up with the love of things present or fear of things to come.

Therefore, *do not be distressed or fearful* (Jn 14:27). Have confidence in Me and trust in My mercy. When you think I am far away, I am often closest to you. When you think that almost all is lost, often a greater reward follows.

All is not lost just because things go contrary to your wishes. Do not judge according to your present feelings, and do not take any trouble so much to heart that you lose all hope of being delivered from it.

4. Do not think you have been completely abandoned because I have sent you some grief, or if I withdraw from you the consolation you longed for; know that this is the way to the kingdom of heaven. No doubt, it is better for you and for the rest of My servants to be tested by adversity than always to have things go your own way.

I know your most hidden thoughts and that it is necessary for your salvation that sometimes you be deprived of spiritual consolation, lest you become too elated with success and, through pride, imagine yourself to be what you really are not. What I have given, I may take away and may restore it again when I please.

5. When I have given something, it is still Mine; when I take it away again, I take nothing that belongs to you, because *every good and perfect gift* (Jas 1:17) belongs to Me.

If I send you trouble or affliction, do not complain nor become depressed. Soon I may lift you up again and turn all your sorrow into joy. Know this: I am just, and all praise is due Me when I deal with you thus.

6. If your thinking is straight and you see things as they really are, you will never allow trouble or adversity to depress you. Rather, you should be glad and give thanks—even considering it a joy that I do not spare you from sorrows.

As the Father has loved Me, so have I loved you (Jn 15:9), I told My beloved disciples; yet I sent them into the world not to have temporal joys, but to fight great battles; not to have honors, but to be despised; not to have ease, but to labor; not to rest, but to bring forth much fruit in patience. Remember these words, My child.

CHAPTER 31

On Disregarding Creatures to Find the Creator

D*ISCIPLE:* Lord, I am much in need of a still greater grace, if I am to arrive at that state where it would be beyond the power of any creature to stand in the way of my progress. As long as anything deters me, I cannot fly freely to You like the person who said: *"If only I had wings like a dove so that I could fly away and be at rest"* (Ps 55:7).

Who can be more at rest than the person of single intention? And who has greater freedom than the person who desires nothing in this world?

JESUS WANTS US TO LIVE FOR HIM—"As the Father has loved Me, so have I loved you. Remain in My love. If you keep My commandments, you will remain in My love, just as I have kept My Father's commandments and remain in His love" (Jn 15:9f).

Persons should, therefore, rise above all creatures and, perfectly forgetting themselves, elevate their minds and see that there is nothing in all creation like You, the Creator of all.

Unless human beings are detached from all created things, they will not be free to make divine things their goal. That is why there are so few contemplatives found who will sever all connections with perishable creatures.

2. A great grace is needed to elevate the soul and lift it above itself. And unless we are so elevated and detached from creatures and completely united to God, our knowledge and our possessions are of little importance.

The one who esteems anything great but Almighty God, the Eternal Good, will remain small in soul and long lie bound to the things of earth. All else besides God is nothing and should be considered as worthless.

There is a vast difference between the wisdom of an enlightened and devout soul and the knowledge of a learned and studious scholar. The knowledge which is poured into the soul by the influence of God's grace is far nobler than that which is acquired by human labor and study.

3. Many are the admirers of contemplation, but few are willing to use the means needed for its attainment. It is a great hindrance to contemplation that we depend so much on outward signs and material things and practice little mortification.

I do not know by what spirit we are led, nor what the aim is of those who are called spiritual persons, that we direct so much of our effort and solicitude toward transitory things, but seldom recollect our senses or give thought to the inward state of our own soul.

4. The sad fact is that after a short period of meditation, we become involved in the external actions of everyday life without pausing to examine our conscience concerning all that we do. We pay no attention where our affections lie, nor do we have sorrow for our lack of pure intention and the sinfulness of our deeds.

In the days of Noah *all the people on earth were perverse in what they did* (Gen 6:12), and therefore God sent the great deluge to destroy it. As long as our intentions are corrupt, so too will be the actions which follow; for they indicate our lack of inward strength. From a clean heart comes the fruit of a good life.

5. Many inquire after the deeds of others, but they have little regard for the zeal and intention with which they did them. They ask whether they are strong, wealthy, handsome, good writers or singers, industrious workers; but whether they are poor in spirit, patient, humble, and live a devout, interior life is of little or no consequence to them.

Nature looks at the exterior of a person, but grace turns itself to the inward intention of the act. Nature is often mistaken, but grace trusts in God and is not deceived.

CHAPTER 32

On Self-Abnegation and the Renunciation of All Covetousness

CHRIST: My child, you cannot have perfect freedom unless you wholly renounce yourself. Those who think only of themselves and are lovers of themselves; the covetous, the curious, the pretentious, the pleasure-seekers—concerned with their own comforts and not the interests of Jesus Christ; those who plan and pursue the things which cannot last—are bound with chains of their own making.

Whatever does not come from God will perish entirely. Keep this brief advice in your mind: Forsake all, and you will find all; relinquish all desire, and you will find rest. If you think this over carefully and put it into practice, you will understand all things.

2. *Disciple:* Lord, this is not the work of one day, nor is it child's play; for in this short sentence is included the whole of religious perfection.

3. *Christ:* My child, when you hear what the way of perfection is, you should not be discouraged or downhearted. Instead, this should be an incentive for you to aim at higher things—or at least to aspire to them.

I would that this were so with you and that you would advance to that state where you were no longer filled with self-love, but would simply wait to do My will and that of the person whom I have set over you. You would please Me greatly, and all your life would pass in joy and peace.

There are still many things you must give up, and unless you give them to Me without reservation, your prayer will not be answered. Therefore, *I advise you to buy from Me gold that has been refined by fire so that you will be truly rich* (Rev 3:18)—that is, heavenly wisdom, which treads underfoot all earthly things. Cast aside worldly wisdom, which seeks to please the world and self.

4. I have told you to acquire what is thought contemptible and worthless by the world, rather than those things which it thinks valuable and desirable. True heavenly wisdom is so cheaply regarded by humans as to be almost forgotten; for this heavenly wisdom goes against nature because it does not hold a high opinion of self, nor does it seek worldly renown.

There are many who praise it with words, but their lives belie their speech. Yet this is *a precious pearl* (Mt 13:46), which is hidden from many because of their presumption.

CHAPTER 33

On Inconstancy of Heart and the Directing of Our Final Intention to God

CHRIST: My child, do not trust your present affections, for they quickly change from one to another. As long as you live, your moods will change, even though you do not will it.

Sometimes you are happy, at other times sad; now you are at peace, then you are upset; at one time devout, at another spiritually dry; sometimes full of vigor, at other times sluggish; one day elated, the next day gloomy.

But those who are wise and have been well instructed in the spiritual life rise above these changing moods, ignoring their inner feelings and on what side the wind of instability blows, so long as the direction of their souls advances toward their desired goal. Thus they can remain stable and unshaken through many changing events, always directing their intention toward Me.

2. The purer your intention is, the greater will be your constancy in weathering these diverse storms. But in many this pure intention is soon dimmed, for they are quick to look for the delightful things which cross their path.

It is rare that you will find anyone completely free from the tarnish of self-seeking. So it was with the Jews who came to Bethany to Martha and Mary—*not just to see Jesus, but in order to see Lazarus* (Jn 12:9) whom He had raised from the dead.

Therefore, your intention must be purified in order to keep it steadfast and simple, directing it to Me despite the various distractions that come between Me and you.

CHAPTER 34

The Person Who Loves God Delights in Him above All Things

DISCIPLE: My God and my all! What more can I have and what more can I desire than You? O sweet and delightful Word! Sweet to him who loves the Word and not the world, nor those things that are in the world.

My God and my all! To the one who understands, enough is said, and yet it is pleasing to the one who loves to say it over again. When You are present, Lord, all things bring delight; but when You are absent, all things are dreary. When You come, You bring peace, joy and gladness, and the heart is at rest.

You give us true judgment in all things and lead us to praise and glorify You in all things. There is no lasting pleasure without You, Lord; but if anything is to be agreeable or pleasant, it can only be with the help of Your grace and it must be seasoned with Your wisdom.

2. Will not all be a delight to those to whom You give a gift? But to those who take no delight in You, what else can be agreeable to them? The worldly-wise and the sensuous are devoid of Your wisdom, for in worldly wisdom is emptiness, and in sensuality is death.

Those, therefore, who follow You, Lord, by despising the world and mortifying the flesh, are wise indeed; for they are led from folly to truth and from the flesh to the spirit. Souls such as these truly love God and refer to Him whatever good is found in creatures.

But what a vast difference between the love of the Creator and that of the creature, between eternity and time, between the uncreated Light and the reflected light of creation!

3. O everlasting Light, surpassing all created light, send down Your bright rays from above to penetrate and illuminate the dark recesses of my heart. Enliven my spirit and all its powers, cleanse it, gladden it and enlighten it, that it may cling to You in joyous rapture.

When will that blessed hour come when You will visit me with the joy of Your presence and be to me my all in all? My joy cannot be full until You grant me this.

But, sorry to say, my old nature still lives within me, for it is not wholly crucified—not perfectly dead. The flesh still lusts strongly against the spirit and, waging war within me, does not permit the kingdom of my soul to be in peace.

4. But You, Who are Lord *over the might of the sea and still the motion of its waves* (Ps 89:10), arise and come to my aid. *Scatter the warring nations* (Ps 68:31) and crush them by Your power.

I beseech You, Lord, to show the strength of Your wonderful works and let the power of Your right hand be glorified; for I have no other hope or refuge but in You, my Lord and my God.

THE ALMIGHTY POWER OF JESUS—"[Jesus] entered the room where the [dead] child was. He took the child by the hand and said to her . . . 'Little girl, I say to you, arise!' And immediately the girl, a child of twelve, got up and began to walk around" (Mk 5:40ff).

CHAPTER 35

On the Lack of Security from Temptation in This Life

CHRIST: My child, you are never secure in this life. As long as you live you will always need spiritual weapons. You are in the midst of enemies, who may attack from the right hand or the left. If you do not make use of the shield of patience on all occasions, it is certain you will be wounded before long.

Moreover, if you do not fix your heart on Me, with the sincere will to endure all things for My sake, you will be unable to stand up under the heat of battle and will fail to win the palm I reserve for My Saints.

Therefore, you must bear all courageously, using a strong hand against all that stands in your way. The person who overcomes is fed with the Bread from heaven, but to the coward is left much misery.

2. If you seek rest in this life, how can you expect to deserve eternal rest? Do not look for rest here, but for much patience. True peace is found only in heaven, not in the human person nor any other creature, but in God alone.

You must be willing to suffer all things gladly for the love of God: labors, sorrows, temptations, afflictions; all anxieties, needs, infirmities, injuries, detraction, rebukes; all humiliations, confusions, corrections, and contempt.

Such things are aids to virtue and test those who are in the service of Christ, preparing them for a heavenly crown. For this short labor I will give an eternal reward, and for passing confusion, infinite glory.

3. Do you believe that spiritual consolations will be yours for the asking? It was not so with My Saints. They had many afflictions and various temptations, and great desolation as well. But they bore up patiently through it all, trusting in God and not themselves; for they considered *the sufferings we presently endure are minuscule in comparison with the glory to be revealed in us* (Rom 8:18).

Do you expect to have here and now what others just managed to obtain after many tears and great labors? *Place your hope in the Lord: be strong and courageous in your heart and place your hope in the Lord* (Ps 27:14). Do not despair, do not give up; but with perseverance offer both body and soul for the glory of God. Your reward will be abundant, and I will be with you in all your tribulations.

CHAPTER 36

Against the Vain Judgments of Humans

CHRIST: *My child, firmly cling to the Lord and do not fear the judgments of humans, when your conscience assures you that you seek to be devout and innocent. Consider it a good thing and rejoice when you suffer that way.

It will not be burdensome to you if you are humble of heart, nor if you trust more in God than in yourself. A lot of people utter many things; therefore attach little importance to what they say.

Neither is it possible to satisfy everybody. St. Paul tried to please everyone in the Lord and became all things to all. Nevertheless, he paid little attention to being judged by humans.

2. He worked for the formation and salvation of others, as much as he could and found possible. In spite of all that, he was unable to prevent others from sometimes judging or despising him.

Therefore he committed everything to God, Who is all-knowing, and put on the armor of patience and humility against the onslaughts of evil tongues, or against those who thought or expressed vain or bad things about him. Sometimes, however, he answered his accusers, when his silence might scandalize the weak.

3. Why be afraid of mortals? A human being is here today and gone tomorrow. Keep up a wholesome fear of God and you will not find it necessary to be afraid of humans. What can others really do against you by words and insults? Those who thus attack you hurt themselves more than you, and wherever they may be, they will not escape God's judgment.

Endeavor to walk always in God's presence and refrain from arguments. And if at times you have been overcome and undeservedly suffer confusion, do not be downcast and do not lessen your future reward by yielding to impatience. But rather look up to Me in heaven, for I am able to

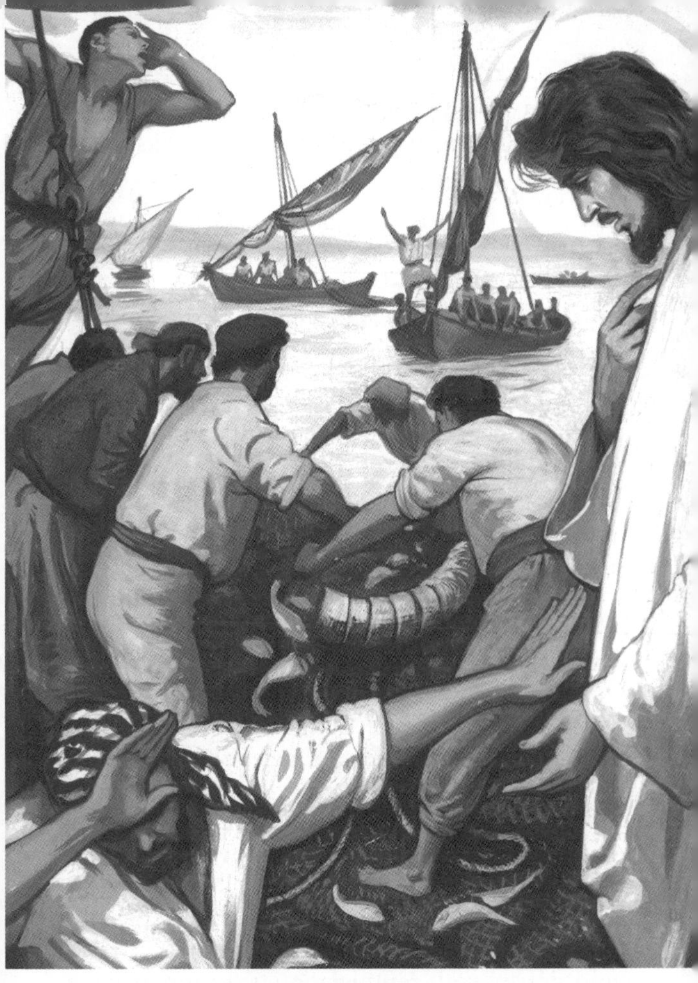

FOLLOWING THE JUDGMENT OF JESUS—"Simon answered, 'Master, we worked hard throughout the night and caught nothing; but if You say so, I will let down the nets.' When they had done this, they caught . . . a great number of fish" (Lk 5:5ff).

deliver you from all trouble and injury, and to repay all persons according to their works.

CHAPTER 37

On Self-Renunciation to Obtain Freedom of Spirit

CHRIST: My child, renounce yourself and you shall find Me. Stand as though you had not the power of choice. Cast out all self-seeking and it will always be to your true advantage; for you will always gain greater grace when you have given yourself up completely to Me without taking back your gift.

2. *Disciple:* Lord, how often must I forsake myself and in what things must I practice self-renunciation?

3. *Christ:* You must forget yourself always and in all things, in small things as well as in those that are great. I make no exceptions, but want you to be divested of your self-will in all things. For how can you be wholly Mine and I totally yours, if you still entertain self-will within and outside yourself?

The sooner you accomplish this, the better will your condition be; and the more complete and sincere your renunciation, the more will you please Me and the greater will be your spiritual gain.

4. There are some who commit themselves, but with some restrictions; for they do not trust

God fully and so they are busy providing for themselves. Some at first give up everything; but afterward, under the pressure of temptation, they return to what they had forsaken; and so they do not advance in virtue.

Such persons will not acquire the true liberty of one who is clean of heart, nor will they obtain the grace of a most joyful familiarity with Me. To attain this, they must first wholly renounce themselves and daily offer themselves as victims of sacrifice to Me; for without this there cannot exist any lasting divine union.

5. I have often told you, and I repeat it again: forsake yourself and renounce yourself, and you shall enjoy great interior peace. Give all for all; seek nothing; take nothing back that you have given up; stand with pure detachment and with full confidence in Me, and then you shall truly possess Me.

Then you shall enjoy true freedom of heart and darkness shall not overcome you. Aim at that alone. Pray for it, desire it, that you may be divested of all self-seeking; and so, spiritually naked, follow the naked Jesus. Thus you will die to yourself and live forever to and for Me.

Then you will be freed from all vain imaginations and from all wicked disturbances and useless cares. Then also, you will no longer yield to unruly fears, and inordinate love will die in you.

CHAPTER 38

On How to Govern Ourselves And on Having Recourse to God in Danger

CHRIST: My child, strive diligently for perfect interior freedom and self-mastery in every place, in every action and occupation, so that you be not the slave of anything, but that all things be under your control.

You must be lord and ruler over your actions, never a bondsman or a mercenary. You must be a free person—similar to a righteous Hebrew—one who is transferred to the rank and the liberty of the children of God. Children of God stand above present things; they contemplate those that are eternal.

They look upon transient things with the left eye; with the right eye they look at heavenly things. They do not allow temporal things to attract them, nor do they cling to them; instead they make those earthly things serve the end and purpose for which God made and ordained them. For the Divine Artist did not leave anything in all His creatures but what is orderly and governed by laws.

2. You, in turn, in all events must not let yourself be ruled by outward appearances, nor be guided by what you see or hear with carnal sentiments. But on every occasion enter, like Moses, into the Tabernacle to consult the Lord.

Then you shall sometimes hear the divine answer and receive instruction for many things

RECOURSE TO JESUS IN TRIALS—"The blind receive their sight, the lame walk, those who have leprosy are cleansed, the deaf hear, the dead are raised to life, the poor have the good news proclaimed to them" (Lk 7:22).

present and to come. For Moses always had recourse to the Tabernacle for resolving doubts and problems. He had recourse to prayer in the presence of dangers and the wickedness of people.

You must act similarly and, seeking shelter in the inmost depths of your heart, earnestly pray for divine help. Recall how Joshua and the children of Israel were misled by the Gibeonites because they did not first consult the Lord, but too easily believed those pleasing words and were taken in by false piety.

CHAPTER 39

On Prudence in Worldly Affairs

CHRIST: My child, always entrust your affairs to Me. In due season, I will dispose such things properly. Wait until I order things and you will recognize it was to your advantage.

2. *Disciple:* Lord, I willingly commit all things to Your care, for my endeavors bring poor profits. I wish that I were less concerned about what the future might bring, but could abandon myself more completely to Your divine pleasure.

3. *Christ:* My child, people frequently pursue a thing they eagerly desire, but when they have achieved it, they begin to see it was a mistake. For our inclinations are unsteady and do not last long, but instead tend to urge us on from one thing to another. For all these reasons it is most important to forsake self, even in the smallest things.

PRUDENCE IN WORLDLY AFFAIRS—"[Jesus] asked them, 'Whose image is this, and whose inscription?' They replied and said to Him, 'Caesar's.' Jesus said to them, 'Give to Caesar what is due to Caesar, and to God what is due to God' " (Mk 12:16f).

4. It is essential for our true spiritual progress that we deny ourselves. And those who have renounced themselves obtain great liberty and enjoy great safety.

The old enemy, however, who wars against everything that is good, does not fail to tempt us. Day and night he uses dangerous tricks to trap the unwary. Hence we are told: *Stay awake and pray that you may not enter into temptation* (Mt 26:41).

CHAPTER 40

We Have No Good of Ourselves and Can Glory in Nothing

DISCIPLE: *What is man that You are mindful of him, the son of man that You care for him?* (Ps 8:5). What does any person have independently of You so as to hold a claim on Your grace? Lord, what reason can I produce to say that You should not forsake me? Or, if You do not grant what I pray for, how can I justify my complaint?

This I may truly think and proclaim: "Lord, I am nothing. There is nothing I can do of myself. There is no good in me as coming solely from myself. On the contrary, I fail; I am defective in everything, and whatever comes from me independently of You tends to nothing. Unless You help me and instruct me, I become lukewarm and slack."

2. Lord, You are always the same and endure forever. You are eternally good, just and holy,

always doing things with goodness, justice and holiness, arranging all things with wisdom.

On the contrary, I am inclined to go backward rather than forward, never remaining stable, but passing through many changes. When it pleases You to give me a helping hand, all at once things improve; for You alone—unaided by human beings—can help me and strengthen me. Then I shall no longer shift from one thing to another, but turn my heart directly to You and rest in You alone.

3. If only I knew well how to dispense with all human comfort, either to attain devotion, or because I am compelled to seek You, since no human being is able to comfort me, then I might justly hope for Your grace and rejoice in Your consolation.

4. As often as things go well with me, I thank You, from Whom all good proceeds. In Your sight I am nothing but an unstable and weak human being; certainly I have nothing to be proud of. Why do I wish people to think well of me, seeing I am but nothingness? This is foolishness.

Vainglory is certainly an evil plague, because it lures us away from true glory and robs us of heavenly grace. When persons are full of pride, they displease You, and when they long for the good opinion of others, they are deprived of true virtue.

5. The only true glory and holy joy is to glory in You, not in self; to rejoice in Your Name, not in one's own virtue, and to find delight in nothing created except for Your sake. May Your Name

be praised, not mine; Your works magnified, not mine.

May Your holy Name be blessed, but let not praises of humans be given to me. You are my glory and the joy of my heart. I will glory and rejoice in You all day. *But about myself I will not boast, except as it concerns my weaknesses* (2 Cor 12:5).

6. Let the unbelievers seek praise from one another; I wish that which is from God alone. All human approbation—in fact, all temporal honor and worldly grandeur—is foolish and meaningless when compared with Your eternal glory. O Truth, O Mercy! O Blessed Trinity, my God! to You be praise, honor and glory, for endless ages of ages!

CHAPTER 41

On the Contempt of All Temporal Things

CHRIST: My child, do not take it to heart if you see others honored and promoted, and yourself despised and looked down upon. Raise up your heart to Me in heaven, and the contempt of people on earth will not sadden you.

2. *Disciple:* Lord, we live in a blind world and are easily and quickly led astray. If I examined myself well, I would find that no creature has ever wronged me, so I have no right to complain against You. Since I have frequently committed grievous sins against You, it is only right that every creature take up arms against me.

Therefore, confusion and contempt are my just portion; while all praise, honor and glory are due to You. Unless I put myself in the frame of mind of being willing to be despised and abandoned by all creatures and to be regarded as nothing, I can be neither inwardly at peace and steadfast, nor wholly united to You.

CHAPTER 42

Our Peace Must Not Depend Upon Human Beings

CHRIST: My child, if to satisfy yourself and to seek the society of any person you place all your contentment in that person, you will become entangled and lose your peace. On the other hand, if you have recourse only to Me, the living and everlasting Truth, you will not be overwhelmed if friends forsake you or you lose them by death.

Whoever they may be, your friends must be loved for My sake, no matter how good they appear to you, or how dear they are to you in this life. No friendship can be profitable or lasting in this life, nor is it a true and pure love which does not have its source in Me.

Your affection toward those you love should be so mortified that you would be willing to be without friends at all. To that degree by which you withdraw from all earthly consolation, such will be your approach to God; and so much higher do you ascend to God, as you lower yourself and become despicable in your own estimation.

2. However, if you attribute anything good to yourself, you only impede God's grace; for the grace of the Holy Spirit ever seeks a humble heart. If only you knew how to forget yourself and to empty yourself of all created love, then would I pour My grace into your heart. The more you look toward creatures, the dimmer becomes the sight of the Creator.

Learn for His sake to overcome yourself in all things, and then you will be able to grow in divine knowledge. No matter how little it is, anything loved and regarded inordinately will keep you back from the supreme Good and corrupt your soul.

CHAPTER 43

On the Vanity of Worldly Learning

CHRIST: My child, do not be impressed by the brilliant and clever sayings of human beings: *the kingdom of God is not a matter of words but of power* (1 Cor 4:20). Listen to My words, which inflame the heart, enlighten the mind, bring repentance for sin to the heart, and infuse it with many consolations.

Reading the Scriptures to appear more learned will not benefit you; but rather study how to overcome your worst faults. This will profit you more than having the answers to difficult questions at your fingertips.

2. When you have read and learned many things, you must necessarily return to the basic fact that I am He Who teaches humans whatever

THE WISDOM OF JESUS—His parents found Jesus in the temple "sitting among the teachers, listening to them and asking them questions. And all who heard Him were amazed at His intelligence and His answers" (Lk 2:46f).

they know; and I give a clearer understanding to the little ones than any person can teach. The person to whom I speak soon becomes wise and quickly advances in the way of the spirit.

But it will go badly for those who curiously inquire after the affairs of humans, and yet give little thought of the way to serve Me. The time will come when I, the Master of teachers and Lord of the Angels, will appear to listen to the accounts of everyone and to examine the conscience of all.

Then will Jerusalem be searched with lanterns and the hidden things of darkness in everyone's soul be brought to light, when all excuses and vain arguments shall be silenced.

3. I am He Who in an instant can so elevate the minds of the humble that they can grasp the reasons for eternal truth more perfectly than others who, lacking humility, have studied ten years in school. For I teach without the sound of words, without conflict of opinions, without striving for honor and without obstinate arguments.

I teach you to despise earthly things, to weary of the things of this present life, to look and to long for what is eternal, to shun honors, to bear injuries patiently, to place complete confidence in Me and, above all, to love Me with all your heart.

4. There was a certain person who, by loving Me with his whole soul, learned the things of God and inspired many by the wonders of the things

he spoke; for he profited more by not pursuing the study of high learning. To some I speak of ordinary things, to others special things; to some I appear in signs and figures, while to others I reveal mysteries in a flood of light.

In books the same voice and the same words appear, but some will get more out of them than others; for it is I alone Who teach the Truth, Who search the hearts—no thoughts are hidden from Me—I, the Prime Mover of all actions, giving to everyone as I see fit.

CHAPTER 44

On Not Drawing to Ourselves Exterior Things

C*HRIST:* It is best for you to be ignorant, My child, about many things, considering yourself as dead to this world, and one to whom all the world is crucified. Let many things you hear go in one ear and out the other, focusing your mind on those things which pertain to your peace.

It is also more profitable for you to look the other way from such things as displease you, leaving to everyone to hold the opinion that seems best, rather than to enter into heated disputes. If you are concerned only with God's view in the matter and are pleasing in His sight, you will consider it a small thing to be worsted in an argument.

2. *Disciple:* Dear Lord, to what a state we have brought ourselves! At a temporal loss we become utterly miserable, toiling and expending much

energy. Whereas, how quickly a spiritual loss is forgotten, and scarcely is ever recalled.

We become all absorbed in those things which profit us little or nothing at all, but our soul's salvation—the thing of vital importance—is negligently passed over. How easily humans tend downward to outward things; but unless they sharply recover themselves, they are content to; dwell on material interests and pleasures.

CHAPTER 45

On Not Being Too Credulous Knowing How Easily We Offend in Speech

D*ISCIPLE:* Help me, O Lord, in my trouble, *for any human assistance is worthless* (Ps 60:13). How often have I relied on the faithfulness of human beings only to be disappointed. Yet how often have I found loyalty where I least expected it!

How foolish, therefore, to put our complete hope in human beings, for it is only in You, dear Lord, that the righteous may trust without fear of betrayal. You, O Lord, are greatly to be blessed in all things that befall us. How weak and unstable we are, and how easily and quickly we are deceived and changed!

2. Who is there who can behave so carefully and prudently in all things as not to be sometimes mistaken or perplexed? Certainly very few. But those who have complete confidence in You, O Lord—seeking You in the simplicity of their hearts—do not slip away from You so easily.

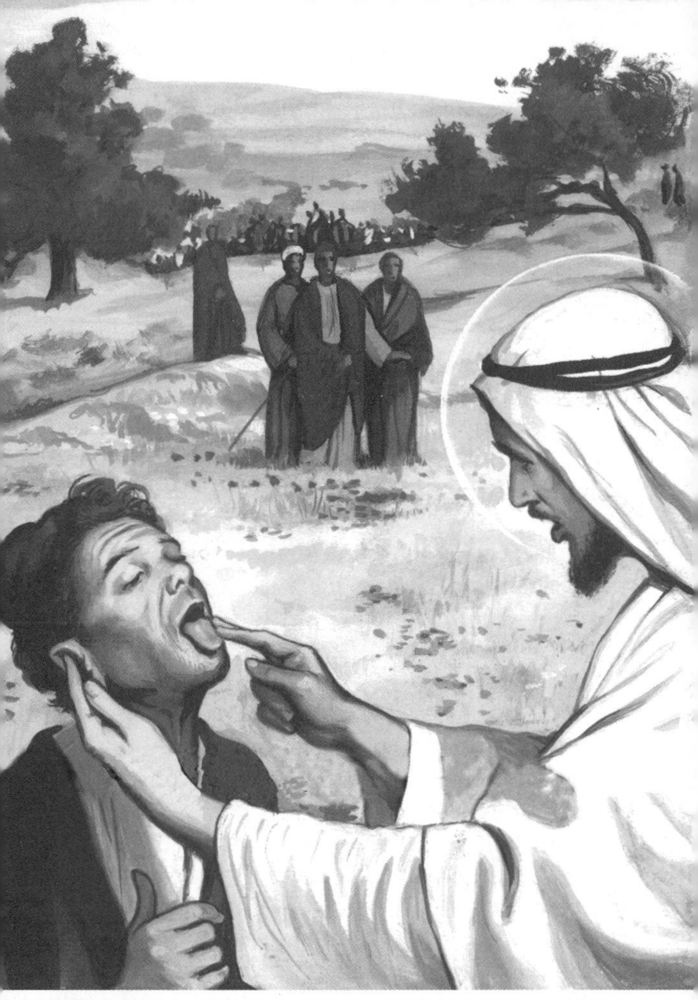

JESUS SANCTIFIES TONGUE AND EARS—"[Jesus] put His fingers into the man's ears and, spitting, touched his tongue. . . . He sighed and said to him, *'Ephphatha!'* which means, 'Be opened!' At once, the man's ears were opened . . . and he spoke properly" (Mk 7:33ff).

And if they should lapse into trouble, no matter how deeply they become involved, You, O Lord, are ever ready to rescue them and comfort them; for You never abandon the soul who completely trusts in You. It is rare indeed that one finds a friend so faithful as to stick with us through thick and thin. You, O Lord, are most faithful in all things and there is none other but You.

3. How wise was the holy St. Agatha, who said: "My mind is solidly established in and grounded upon Christ!" If only this were so with me, I would not be a prey to so many fears and anxieties, nor would the unkind words of others move me.

There is no one who can foresee future events or take precautions against future disasters. If even approaching evils can hurt us, how much greater the wound of those unlooked for? But why have I not made better provision for my wretched self? And why have I so readily put my trust in others? Truly because we are frail and weak human beings, though many think of and speak of us as Angels.

In whom can I believe, O Lord, except in You? For You alone are the Truth, Who can neither deceive nor be deceived. On the other hand, *all people are liars* (Ps 116:11), weak, unstable and subject to fail, especially in speech; so that even what seems to be true we should not be too ready to believe.

4. You wisely have warned us to be on our guard against human beings, that often *one's ene-*

THE HOLY ROSARY

PRAYER BEFORE THE ROSARY

QUEEN of the Holy Rosary, you have deigned to come to Fatima to reveal to the three shepherd children the treasures of grace hidden in the Rosary. Inspire my heart with a sincere love of this devotion, in order that by meditating on the Mysteries of our Redemption which are recalled in it, I may be enriched with its fruits and obtain peace for the world, the conversion of sinners and of Russia, and the favor which I ask of you in this Rosary. *(Here mention your request.)* I ask it for the greater glory of God, for your own honor, and for the good of souls, especially for my own. Amen.

The Five Joyful Mysteries

Said on Mondays and Saturdays [except during Lent], and the Sundays from Advent to Lent.

1. The Annunciation
For the love of humility.

2. The Visitation
For charity toward my neighbor.

3. The Nativity
For the spirit of poverty.

4. The Presentation
For the virtue of obedience.

5. Finding in the Temple
For the virtue of piety.

The Five Sorrowful Mysteries

Said on Tuesdays and Fridays throughout the year, and every day from Ash Wednesday until Easter.

1. Agony in the Garden
For true contrition.

2. Scourging at the Pillar
For the virtue of purity.

3. Crowning with Thorns
For moral courage.

4. Carrying of the Cross
For the virtue of patience.

5. The Crucifixion
For final perseverance.

The Five Glorious Mysteries

Said on Wednesdays [except during Lent], and the Sundays from Easter to Advent.

1. The Resurrection
For the virtue of faith.

2. The Ascension
For the virtue of hope.

3. Descent of the Holy Spirit
For love of God.

4. Assumption of the B.V.M.
For devotion to Mary.

5. Crowning of the B.V.M.
For eternal happiness.

The Five Luminous Mysteries

Said on Thursdays [except during Lent].

1. The Baptism of Jesus
For living my Baptismal Promises.

2. Christ's Self-Manifestation at Cana
For doing whatever Jesus says.

3. Proclamation of the Kingdom
For seeking God's forgiveness.

4. The Transfiguration
Becoming a New Person in Christ.

5. Institution of the Eucharist
For active participation at Mass.

PRAYER AFTER THE ROSARY

O GOD, Whose, only-begotten Son, by His Life, Death, and Resurrection, has purchased for us the rewards of eternal life; grant, we beseech You, that, meditating upon these Mysteries of the Most Holy Rosary of the Blessed Virgin Mary, we may imitate what they contain and obtain what they promise, through the same Christ our Lord. Amen.

℣. May the divine assistance remain always with us. ℟. Amen.

℣. And may the souls of the faithful departed, through the mercy of God, rest in peace. ℟. Amen.

THE NEW LUMINOUS MYSTERIES

THE new Mysteries, i.e., Mysteries of Light or the Luminous Mysteries, suggested by Pope John Paul II, are intended to offer contemplation on important parts of Christ's Public Life in addition to the contemplation on His Childhood, His Sufferings, and His Risen Life offered by the traditional Mysteries.

The Pope assigned these new Mysteries to Thursday while transferring the Joyful Mysteries—normally said on that day—to Saturday because of the special Marian presence in them.

mies will be the members of his own household (Mt 10:36), and that we are to be wary if anyone should tell us: *" 'Look, here is the Messiah,' or 'There He is' "* (Mt 24:23). This I have learned at great expense and I hope it will make me more cautious in the future.

Those who confide their secrets to others, cautioning them not to repeat them to a soul, often cannot keep their own secrets, but betray both themselves and their confidants. From such foolish talk and such imprudent people, defend me, O Lord, that I become not their victim, or commit the same fault.

Grant that my words be true and constant, and drive far from me a sly and malicious tongue. What I am unwilling to endure, I certainly ought to use all means to avoid myself.

5. How good and peaceful it is to remain silent about other people's words and deeds, not to believe without proof all that is said, nor lightly to repeat all we see or hear. We should open our own hearts to very few; for it is better to seek You, Lord, Who can see into every person's heart.

It is not for us to be wafted about by every wind of words, but rather to hope that both our interior and our outward life may be lived according to Your holy will. In order to possess heavenly grace, let us shun as far as we can all worldly conversation, not desiring what appears outwardly pleasant and agreeable, but diligently following those things which bring amendment of life and fervor.

A virtue that has been known and praised too hastily has harmed many a soul, while one kept in silence has proved beneficial in this uncertain life of temptation and warfare.

CHAPTER 46

On Putting Our Trust in God When Evil Words Are Spoken against Us

C*HRIST:* My child stand firm and trust in Me. What are words but only wind? They fly through the air, but hurt not a stone upon the ground.

If you are innocent, then you will gladly suffer such words for the love of God. If, on the other hand, you are guilty, determine willingly to make amends. It is a small matter for you to put up with a few words uttered in haste when you are yet unable to bear hard blows.

It is because you are still worldly and are eager to please others that you take such little things to heart. When you resent being corrected for your faults and seek shelter in excuses, it is because you are afraid of being despised. Search your soul carefully and you will discover that the world is still strong in you, as well as that impossible desire to please others.

2. For when you dread to be abased and humiliated for faults, it is clear that you are not truly humble, nor dead to the world, nor is the world crucified to you. Just listen to My word and

you will not mind even if ten thousand people speak against you.

Even if all the evils, which the worst human malice can invent, were said against you, what harm can they possibly do you if you pay no attention to them? They cannot take so much as one hair from your head.

3. But if you do not keep your eyes fixed on God, nor keep Him in your heart, then you will be easily upset by the slightest rebuke. Those who trust in Me and rely not on their own judgment will fear no human. For I am the Judge and the Discerner of all secrets.

I know how everything is done, and I know both the one who inflicts the injury and the one whom it affects. Nothing happens without My permission and the power so to act, *that out of many hearts thoughts may be revealed* (Lk 2:35). I will judge both the guilty and the innocent, but I will test them both beforehand.

4. Human judgment is often erroneous. My judgment is true; it shall stand and can never be overthrown. To many it remains hidden, and only to a few is it made manifest; yet it never errs, nor can it err, though to the unwise it may appear wrong. So when you need to make a decision, always come to Me and do not rely upon your own judgment.

Righteous persons are never dismayed by anything I permit to happen to them. Although they be wrongly accused, it will not worry them much; neither will they be overjoyed if they be reasonably acquitted. They know that *I am the searcher of all hearts* (Rev 2:23), Who judge not according to outward appearances or by the way things look to humans, but by what I esteem praiseworthy.

5. *Lord, God, most just Judge* (Ps 7:12), strong and patient, You know the frailty and the malice of human beings. I beseech You to be my strength and my guide, for my conscience of itself is not sufficient. You know what I do not know, and that even under reprimand I ought to humble myself and bear it meekly. For as often as I have not acted thus, in Your great mercy forgive me and give me the grace of greater endurance for the future.

The torrent of Your mercy is the surer and more profitable way for me to obtain Your forgiveness than my protesting the innocence of my inmost conscience. Although *my conscience may not accuse me of any fault* (1 Cor 4:4), thereby I am not justified. For if You withhold Your mercy, *no one living is righteous* (Ps 143:2).

CHAPTER 47

All Grievous Things Are to Be Borne for the Sake of Eternal Life

CHRIST: My child let not the labors which you have undertaken for My sake crush you; nor let any trouble cause you to lose heart. For whatever happens, have confidence that My promise will be your strength and consolation. I will reward you beyond all limits and measure.

JESUS CAN OVERCOME ALL TRIALS—"Jesus responded, 'Amen, amen, I say to you, before Abraham began to exist, I AM!' On hearing this, they picked up stones to throw at Him, but Jesus hid Himself and left the temple" (Jn 8:58f).

Your labor here will not be of long duration and you shall not always be oppressed with sorrows. Wait a little while and you will see an end to all your troubles. The hour will come sooner than you think when toil and trial shall be no more; for all that passes with time is short-lived and counts but little.

2. Continue on with what you are doing; labor perseveringly in My vineyard, and *I Myself will be your reward* (Gen 15:1). Continue your writing, reading, singing, lamenting, keeping silence and praying, and bearing your troubles bravely; for eternal life is worth all these combats and more.

Peace shall come at a time known only to the Lord. And it will not last a day or a night as we calculate time; there will be light everlasting, infinite glory, unbroken peace and undisturbed rest.

Then you will not say: "What a wretch I am! *Who will rescue me from this body destined for death?*" (Rom 7:24). Nor shall you cry out: "*Why have I been doomed as an exile?*" (Ps 120:5). For death shall be no more and health of body and soul shall never end; neither shall there be anxiety, but only blessed joy and the enjoyable companionship of heaven.

3. Oh! if we could only see the unfading crowns of the Saints in heaven and in what great glory they now rejoice—they whom the world once scorned and thought hardly fit to live; with what alacrity we would humble ourselves to the dust, eager to be subject to all than to lord it over even one person.

You would not seek the pleasures of this life, but rather would be glad to suffer here for God's sake, esteeming it a great advantage to be thought nothing of by human beings.

4. If you were really eager to get to heaven, you would relish with joy the struggles and conflicts of this world, never daring even once to complain; knowing in your inmost heart that where I am with all My Saints, here in the kingdom of My Father, is where you will remain safe and at rest after your tribulations in this world are at an end.

CHAPTER 48

On the Day of Eternity and the Troubles of This Life

DISCIPLE: O blessed mansion of the heavenly city! How bright is the day of eternity! There no darkness ever obscures, for God, the high Truth, illumines and makes all clear. Day is always joyful, always secure and never changes to the contrary.

Oh, how I long for that day to shine upon me, when all temporal things will come to an end! That blessed day indeed shines upon the Saints with everlasting clarity, while we earthly pilgrims perceive it only as a distant goal, seen only through a dark glass.

2. The heavenly citizens know how full of joy that day is, but we poor banished children of Eve know full well the bitterness, and how tedious are the days of our earthly exile. These days are short indeed, but full of evil, sorrow and trouble.

We are often defiled by many sins, enmeshed in our own passions, disquieted by a multitude of fears, overwhelmed with unceasing cares, distracted with curiosities and endless vanities, blinded by errors, burdened by labors which wear us down, vexed by temptations, weakened by worldly pleasures and sometimes tormented by poverty and want.

3. When will there be an end of these miseries? When shall we be set free from the bondage of sin and vice?

When, O Lord, will You occupy all my thoughts so that I find in You my full measure of joy? When shall I live in true liberty, free of the impediments of mind and body? Above all, when will be that peace so desired by all human beings—firm and undisturbed within and without, secure on all sides?

O dear Jesus, when shall I behold You face to face, to stand and contemplate the glory of Your kingdom? When will You be all in all to me?

Oh, when will I be in Your kingdom which from all eternity You have prepared for those who love You? For now I am bereft, poor and exiled in the enemy's country, faced with the battles of daily life which threaten to make me fail You.

4. Comfort me in my exile, ease my sorrow, for to You I cry out with longing. For the comforts of this world can only be a burden to me, since all I long to enjoy is the intimate possession of You, even though now this is unattainable.

Although my desire is to cling to heavenly things, yet I am dragged down by my unmortified passions. My mind wishes to rise above these things, but the weakness of my flesh drags me down against my will. Unhappy person that I am, I fight with myself and *am a burden to myself* (Job 7:20), while at one and the same time, my spirit tends upward and my flesh ever seeks the things below.

5. What inward suffering is mine, while my mind would think of heavenly things and my prayers are interrupted by a host of carnal thoughts! O dear God, *do not remain far from me and depart not from Your servant in anger* (Ps 27:9). Send the light of Your grace and dispel all carnal thoughts from me.

Let the lightning of Your love come with all speed to put to flight the strategy of the enemy. Grant that my senses may be recollected in You, so that I may forget all worldly desires. Help me, O Divine Truth, and purify all my motives. When You send Your heavenly sweetness, every impurity will flee before Your face.

In Your great mercy forgive me also all those times that I think of anything besides You in time of prayer; for I must confess—and You well know it, Lord—that I am usually very distracted. So often my thoughts are miles away from where my body stands or sits and these thoughts are mostly occupied with the things I love; the things I most readily think of are things that are pleasant to nature and the product of habit.

6. But You, O Eternal Truth, have plainly told us: *"Where your treasure is, there will your heart also be"* (Mt 6:21). So, if I love heaven, I love to think of heavenly things; but if I love the world, I rejoice at its prosperity and grieve over its adversity.

If I love the spirit, I delight to think of spiritual things; but if I love the flesh, my imagination is occupied with the delights of the flesh. So whatever is uppermost in my affections, these I willingly listen to and speak of, and carry the thoughts of them often in my mind.

Blessed are those who abandon all things for love of You, O Lord, who overcome their nature and, through fervor of spirit, crucify the lusts of the flesh. Then with a serene conscience they may offer pure prayer to You, and at last become worthy to join the choirs of the holy Angels, having shut out all the internal and external things of this world.

CHAPTER 49

On the Longing for Eternal Life and How Great Are the Joys Promised to Those Who Fight to Gain That Life

C*HRIST:* My child, when you feel the desire for eternal happiness given to you from above, so that you wish to abandon this mortal body in order to behold clearly and without any shadow the brightness of My glory, open wide your heart, and with all the desire of your soul receive this holy inspiration.

Give greatest thanks to the good God, Who deals so generously with you, mercifully visits you, fervently stirs you and powerfully raises you up, so that you do not revert back to the things of earth.

It is not by your own thought or effort that you attain this, but only through the gift of grace and God's loving regard for you; so that you will grow in humility and virtue and prepare yourself for future conflicts, to labor with all the love of your heart to remain faithfully close to Me.

2. The fire often burns, my child, but a flame never shoots up without smoke. And so it is in the spiritual life: the desires of some are aflame after heavenly things, but they are not yet free from the smoke of worldly desires.

Thus they do not act purely for God's glory when they make their petitions to Him. Such often is the way of your own desire which you try to persuade Me is so urgent, for it is so often mixed with self-interest.

3. Do not ask for what is expedient and agreeable to you, but what is acceptable and pleasing in My sight. If you judge correctly, you will prefer My commands and My will in preference to the fulfillment of your own desires, and before all things that you can desire besides Me.

I know all your desires, and I have heard your many petitions. You would like to be enjoying already the freedom and the glory of the children of God, basking in the sunshine of your eternal home and the supreme happiness of the heavenly country.

But that hour has not yet come, for you are still living in another time—a time of war, of toil and of probation. You long to be filled with the Supreme Good, but you cannot have it now. It is I, the Lord; wait for Me until the kingdom of God comes.

4. You must still be tried here on earth and tested in many ways. Sometimes you will receive consolation, but never to your entire satisfaction. *Take courage and be strong* (Deut 31:7), whether in doing or in suffering things repugnant to nature. You must be changed into a new person, often doing what you would not do and leaving undone what you would like to do.

Other people's interests will prosper, but your own will not succeed; others will be listened to, but people will pay no attention to what you say. Others will ask and shall receive, but your requests will be refused.

5. Often people will say nice things about others, but never a good word about you. Others will be promoted to positions of trust, but you will be judged unfit.

Naturally, this kind of things goes against the grain; but if you bear it in silence, you will advance considerably. For these—and many like things—are means by which the faithful servants of the Lord are tried, in order to determine how far they can deny and break their own will in all things.

There is nothing that you need so much as to die to self by seeing and suffering those things that are contrary to your own will—especially when the things commanded seem not only inconvenient, but utterly senseless. Because you are under obedience you dare not resist superior authority, and therefore it is harder to be at the direction of another and to give up your own opinion entirely.

6. But think, My child, of the fruit of these hardships and what they will win for you; how soon they will end, when you will feel no more grief or pain, but the sweetest consolation of the Holy Spirit for your goodwill. In return for the weak will you freely surrender now, you will always have your own will in heaven; for there you will possess all good without fear of losing it.

There your will—always at one with Mine—will desire nothing for yourself alone apart from My desires. No one will resist you there, no one complain about you, and no one stand in your way. Every desirable good will be present simultaneously and all your powers of loving will be filled to the very brim.

There I will give you glory for the affronts you have endured, a robe of honor for your desolation, and a seat in My kingdom forever instead of the lowest place here. There your obedience will be rewarded, the toil of penance turned into joy, and humble submission receive a crown of glory.

7. During this present life, therefore, act humbly toward all people, paying no attention to

who says this or who orders that; so that whether it be your superior, your equal, or one in lower rank, you accept it all with good grace, and with sincere goodwill strive to perform it.

Let one person seek this, another that; let this person exult in one thing, another in something else, and be praised any number of times. As for you, let your contentment be solely in what pleases Me and for My honor alone. Your greatest desire must be—whether in life or in death—that God may be always glorified in you.

CHAPTER 50

How Persons Who Are Desolate Ought to Offer Themselves into the Hands of God

D*ISCIPLE:* Lord God, most holy Father, be You blessed now and forever! As You will, so has it been done—what You do is always for the best. Let Your servant rejoice in You—not in myself or any other, but in You; for You alone are my true happiness. You are my hope and my crown, Lord, my joy and my honor.

What do I possess, O Lord, that I have not received from You—and that without any merit of my own? All things are Yours, both what You have given and what You have made. *Since infancy I have been wretched and close to death* (Ps 88:16). Often my heart is so sad that I am moved to tears, and sometimes my soul is disturbed within itself because of the many passions that come from the world and the flesh.

2. Lord, how I long for the joy of inward peace, that peace enjoyed by Your chosen children, who are nourished by You in the light of Your consolation. O Lord, if You infuse Your peace and holy joy, my soul shall be full of melody and sing Your praises.

But if You withdraw from me, as You must often do, I will be unable to follow in the way of Your commandments; but, rather, on bended knees I shall beat my breast, because things are not the same with me now as they were before, when Your lamp shone over my head and the shadow of Your wings protected me from the temptations which assailed me.

3. O just Father, holy and ever to be praised, the hour has come for Your servant to be tested. It is truly fitting that I should suffer something for You.

Most honored Father, You foresaw from all eternity that for a short time I would be outwardly oppressed, being despised as little in the eyes of the world, but living interiorly always for You, so that I might rise again from my afflictions, sufferings and weaknesses in the dawn of a new light, and be glorified in heaven with You.

Holy Father, You have so appointed it and willed it so, and that which You have ordained has come to pass.

4. Indeed, this is the way You show favor to Your friends: You permit them to suffer and meet with trials in this world, to prove their love for You. How often and by whom You permit

this to happen is all determined by Your Divine Providence. All is governed by Your laws and nothing happens by chance.

It was a blessing for me to be afflicted, so that I might learn Your decrees (Ps 119:71), and cast away all pride and presumption. It is good for me to have known disgrace, that I may learn from it to look for help and assistance from You rather than from human beings. I have also learned to fear Your unsearchable judgments, for You afflict the good person as well as the wicked, but not without equity and justice.

5. I thank You, O heavenly Father, that You have not spared my sins, that Your rod of correction has taught me by inflicting pains and by sending afflictions both within and without. You are the heavenly Physician, Who alone can comfort me, Who—in the midst of wounds—heals, *Who casts down to the depths of the netherworld and brings up from the great abyss* (Tob 13:2). Your tender care is upon me, and your very rod shall instruct me.

6. I am in Your hands, O most loving of Fathers. Strike me where You will that I may bend my perversity to Your will. Make me a humble and pious pupil, that I may walk according to Your direction. I offer myself and all that is mine for Your correction; for it is better to be punished here than in the world to come.

You know all and no one's conscience is hidden from Your eyes. You know the future before it happens; and there is no need for anyone to tell

JESUS, LORD OF NATURE—"Then [Jesus] said, 'Young man, I say to you, arise!' The dead man sat up and began to speak, and Jesus gave him to his mother" (Lk 7:14f).

You what is happening on earth. You know what is needful for my progress and how to make use of trials to remove from me the rust of sin. Therefore, do with me as You will; and despise not my sinful life, known to no one better or more clearly than to You alone.

7. Grant me, O Lord, to know what I ought to know, to love what I ought to love, to esteem what is valuable to You, and to loathe what is vile in Your eyes. Let me never judge according to outward appearances, nor pass judgment on the hearsay of the unwise.

Matters both visible and spiritual are to be determined with right judgment; and above all let me ever seek Your goodwill and pleasure.

8. People's senses often lead them to make wrong decisions and erroneous judgments. The lovers of this world are deceived and love only what they see. How is a person any better by being thought so by another? For one deceitful person deceives another, the blind mislead the blind, and the weak mislead the weak.

Certain it is that persons often confuse others whom they vainly praise. Said the humble St. Francis: "Whatever persons are worth in the sight of God, that they are and no more."

CHAPTER 51

On Exercising Ourselves in Humble Works When We Cannot Attain to the Highest

CHRIST: My child, you cannot always have a burning desire for holiness, nor remain constantly in a high degree of contemplation; but because of fallen nature, you must sometimes descend to lower things and shoulder the burden of this corruptible life, even though you dislike it and find it wearisome.

For as long as we are contained within this mortal body, we experience weariness and heaviness of heart. As long as you are in the flesh, you should often regret its burden, since it prevents you from giving all your time to spiritual exercises and divine contemplation.

2. At such times it is better for you to undertake humble, exterior works and to restore your inner strength in doing good deeds.

Then await My coming with a steady trust; bear patiently your exile and your spiritual dryness, until My heavenly visitation delivers you from all that torments you. Then will you forget your troubles as I fill you with My inward peace.

Then will I spread open before you the delightful fields of Holy Scripture, that with your heart enlarged, you may quickly run in the way of My commandments. Then you will say: *I consider that the sufferings we presently endure are minuscule in comparison with the glory to be revealed in us* (Rom 8:18).

CHAPTER 52

That Persons Ought to Think That They Do Not Deserve Consolation But Rather Punishment

DISCIPLE: Lord, I am not worthy to have Your consolation or any spiritual visitation.

You deal justly with me, therefore, when You leave me forsaken and desolate. For could I shed tears to fill the sea, still I would be unworthy of Your consolation. You know how grievously and in how many things I have sinned against You, so as to deserve nothing but punishment and pain.

According to all justice, I do not deserve Your least consolation. But it is not Your will, O Lord, that what You have created should perish; and it is because of Your mercy and Your pity, O my God, that You grant to your servant—beyond all deserts—to experience the richness of Your loving kindness.

I cannot recall a single good that I have done that You should stoop from heaven to comfort Your servant—beyond all human comprehension—because Your consolation is very different from the empty words of humans.

2. What have I done, O Lord, that You should bestow any heavenly comfort on me? I have always been prone to sin and slow to make amends. Certainly this truth I cannot deny; for if I should say otherwise, You would stand to accuse me and there would be no one to defend me.

Truly, my sins have deserved nothing but hell and everlasting damnation. Frankly, I deserve nothing but scorn and contempt, for I am not fit to be numbered among Your devout servants. And though it is painful for me to admit this, yet, for the sake of truth, I must accuse myself of all my sins, with the hope that I may the more readily deserve to obtain Your merciful forgiveness.

3. Of course I am guilty and full of shame and confusion. What else can I say but that I have sinned, Lord, I have sinned? Have mercy on me and pardon me. *Let me alone so that I may have a few moments of happiness before I go to the land of gloom and deep darkness, never again to return* (Job 10:20-21).

What do You ask most, Lord, of a poor guilty sinner except repentance and self-abasement for personal sins? For true contrition and a humble heart bring forth hope of forgiveness, the troubled conscience is reconciled, and the grace that was lost is recovered and a person is secured against the wrath to come. God and the penitent soul meet together with a holy kiss.

4. Humble contrition of heart is a most acceptable sacrifice to You, O Lord, which is more fragrant than burning incense. It is that sweet ointment which You welcomed to have poured over Your sacred feet; for *a contrite and humble heart, O God, You will not spurn* (Ps 51:19). There is the place of refuge from the wrath of the enemy; there whatever has been defiled is washed away.

CHAPTER 53

God's Grace Is Incompatible with the Love of Worldly Things

C*HRIST:* My child, My grace is precious and will not be mingled with earthly things or worldly consolation. You must get rid of every impediment if you would have that priceless gift poured into your soul.

Choose a hidden place for yourself and delight to retire there alone, where you need not talk with anyone, but instead pour out your heart to God in prayer. In this way you will have a clear conscience and a contrite heart. Look upon the whole world as nothing, preferring to give your time to God before all external things.

You cannot fix your mind on Me and at the same time delight in transitory pleasures. Friends and acquaintances must be kept at a distance and your heart disengaged from all temporal comfort. This is what the blessed Apostle St. Peter beseeches the faithful of Christ: to keep themselves as *aliens and exiles* (1 Pet 2: 11) in this world.

2. When people are about to depart from this world, what confidence will be theirs at that moment if they are not detained by an attachment to anything in this world! But a weak soul is yet incapable of detaching its heart perfectly from all things; nor can the carnal person understand the liberty of the spiritual person.

Persons who would be truly spiritual must renounce both those who are near as well as those who are far away; and they must especially beware of themselves, for in overcoming themselves, they will the more easily subdue all things else. The most noble and perfect victory is the triumph over oneself.

Therefore, persons who keep themselves in subjection so that their sensuality obeys their reason, and their reason is obedient to Me in all

JESUS ENTRUSTS HIMSELF INTO THE FATHER'S HANDS—"It was now about noon, and darkness came over the whole land. . . . Jesus cried out, 'Father, into Your hands I commend My spirit.' And with these words He breathed His last" (Lk 23:44, 46).

things, are indeed, the true conquerors of themselves and the lords of the world.

3. If you would climb to this height of spirituality, you must begin heroically by laying the axe to the root in order to cut away and destroy utterly those secret and uncontrolled inclinations toward yourself and toward every personal and material gain.

From this vice of self-love emanates almost all that must be uprooted and overcome. Once this has been mastered and brought under control, you will know a great peace and tranquility.

But there are few who endeavor to die completely to themselves and to rise above their own nature. Therefore they are so centered on themselves as to make it almost impossible to be lifted in spirit above themselves.

Persons who really desire to walk freely with Me must mortify all their evil and unnecessary affections and must not cling selfishly to anything created.

CHAPTER 54

On the Opposition between Nature and Grace

CHRIST: My child, carefully observe the actions of nature and grace, for both move in opposite directions and in such subtle ways as to be indistinguishable except by the spiritually enlightened. All human beings long after goodness and pretend there is some good in what they say or do; that is why many are deceived by an apparent goodness.

2. Nature indeed is wily and betrays many through its deceits and crafty ways, and has always self as its end. On the other hand, grace walks with simplicity, turning aside from all that appears evil. It employs no deceits, but does all unaffectedly, purely for God, in Whom it rests.

3. Nature dies hard and is not easily overcome or repressed. Never under its own accord will it be subject to obedience.

But grace studies how to be mortified to both the world and the flesh, desires to be overcome and under obedience, and seeks not its own liberty, nor to dominate any creature. Grace always wants to live under God's direction, and for His sake to place itself humbly under every human creature.

4. Nature always looks to its own advantage, considering what gain it can derive from another. But grace is not concerned with its own profit, but with what may benefit others.

5. Nature looks for honor and respect. Grace refers all honor and reverence to God.

6. Nature fears rebukes and contempt. Grace is happy to suffer them for the Name of Jesus.

7. Nature craves ease and idleness. But grace cannot be idle and gladly embraces toil.

8. Nature surrounds itself with rare and costly things and looks down upon what is coarse and cheap. Grace takes joy in humble and simple

things, does not disdain hard things, nor refuses to be clad in poor clothing.

9. Nature focuses its attention on worldly matters, is elated by material gains, is downcast by losses, and is cut to the quick by a sharp word. Grace is intent upon things eternal, is not worried by the loss of things, nor grieved by the unkind word; for its treasure and joy are in heaven, where nothing is lost.

10. Nature is greedy and gladly takes rather than gives, and clings possessively to private possessions. But grace is kind and unselfish, avoids self-interest, is content with little, and rightly judges that *it is more blessed to give than to receive* (Acts 20:35).

11. Nature is inclined to seek creatures, to the love of its own flesh, to idle pastimes and to unnecessary running about. Grace draws people toward the love of God and virtuous living, renounces all created things, flees the world, despises the lusts of the flesh, restrains all useless wanderings, and avoids as much as possible appearing in public.

12. Nature gladly receives exterior comfort to gratify the senses. Grace seeks comfort only in God, finding delight in the Sovereign Good beyond all things visible.

13. Nature does everything for personal profit, never doing any work for nothing, but always looking for repayment—at least in equal amount, if not better, or else for praise and favor—and longs to have its deeds and words highly valued.

On the other hand, grace seeks no temporal reward nor any other compensation in payment, but only God Himself. Grace will have no more of the necessities of life than that which serves to obtain everlasting life.

14. Nature enjoys having a crowd of relatives and friends, prides itself on the family tree and a distinguished background. Nature flatters the rich and caters to those in power and approves those who share the same opinions as itself.

But grace behaves differently, for it loves even its enemies, and does not boast of having a large circle of friends. It cares not for rank or birth unless joined with greater virtue. It favors the poor rather than the rich; and has more in common with the simple and the innocent than with the influential.

It rejoices with the truthful and not with liars. It encourages the good to be zealous to aim higher, and by the exercise of virtues to become more like Christ, our Lord.

15. As soon as trouble and want appear, nature is quick to complain. Grace gladly bears poverty with constancy.

16. Nature refers all things to itself and all its striving is for itself but grace refers all things back to God, Who is their Source. Grace is not presumptuous and attributes no good to self; neither does grace argue or prefer its own opinions, but submits to Eternal Wisdom.

17. Nature wants to know secrets and is avid for news, wants to appear in public and to try out

new things. It likes to be noticed and to do sensational things to win approval. Grace cares nothing for the novel or curious, for it knows that all this springs from our old corruption, since there is nothing new or lasting upon earth.

Grace teaches us to control our senses, to shun all vain pleasure and outward show, and humbly to hide anything that might win human admiration. In all knowledge and in all actions, grace seeks not only spiritual profit, but, above all, the praise and honor of God, that He may be blessed in His gifts, which He freely bestows through His love.

18. This grace is a supernatural light and a special gift of God. It is the proper mark of the elect and a pledge of eternal salvation. It lifts a person above the things of earth to the love of heavenly things, making a spiritual person of a worldling.

The more nature is kept down and overcome, the more grace fills a human soul, and through new daily visitations the soul is formed more and more to the image of God.

CHAPTER 55

On the Corruption of Nature and the Power of God's Grace

DISCIPLE: O Lord, my God, You have made me in Your own image and likeness; grant me this grace which You have shown me to be so great and so necessary for my salvation: to overcome my corrupt nature, which drags me down to sin and the loss of my soul.

In my flesh I see the law of sin opposing the law of my mind, leading me into bondage; so that I incline more toward giving in to my sensual inclinations, nor am I able to resist these passions unless Your holy grace comes to my aid, infusing its fervor into my heart.

2. In order to overcome nature, I need Your grace in great abundance, for this nature of ours is ever prone to evil even from its youth. For it was defiled by sin through the first man, Adam, and the penalty of that stain has descended upon all humankind.

To think that the very nature You made so good and upright is now captured for sin and corruption to the extent that its purely natural inclinations always draws us toward evil and base desires! And so the little strength and inclination to good still remaining are as a small spark of fire hidden among the ashes. This is our natural reason which—though surrounded by much darkness—is still able to discern good from evil and the true from the false. Yet it is unable to carry out all it approves, nor does it possess the full light of truth, or its former wholesome affections.

3. Hence it is, O my God, that *inwardly in my soul I take delight in Your law* (Rom 7:22) and in Your teaching; for I know what You command is good, just and holy, both for the reproval of all evil and for the avoidance of all sin. Yet when I

prefer to obey my senses rather than my reason, *I serve the law of sin* (Rom 7:25).

From this it follows that *though I will to do good, because of my weakness I fail to accomplish it* (Rom 7:18). Thus I often make good resolutions, but because grace is lacking to me, in my weakness I often turn back and yield to the slightest resistance.

I know the way of perfection and can see clearly what I ought to do. But weighed down by the burden of my corruption, I do not rise to heights of greater perfection.

4. Dear Lord, how absolutely necessary is Your grace for me, not only to begin that which is good, but to persevere with it and to accomplish it. Without You, I can do nothing, but when Your grace strengthens me, I can do all things.

O grace, without which our own merits are worthless and the gifts of nature valueless, truly it is from heaven that this comes to us! There are no arts, beauty, strength or riches, no ability or eloquence—none of these can help me, Lord, unless accompanied by Your grace. After all, nature's gifts are common to all human beings, both good and bad. But grace—or Your love—is given only to the elect, and those who are so marked are made worthy to attain the kingdom of heaven.

So excellent is this grace that no other gift—whether it be prophecy, the working of miracles, or the highest and most sublime contemplation—is worth anything without it. Not even faith and hope or any other virtues are acceptable to You without charity and grace.

5. O blessed grace, that makes the poor in spirit rich in virtue, and makes those who are endowed with worldly goods humble of heart, come and descend into my soul and fill me with Your consolation, lest my soul faint because of its own weariness and dryness!

I beseech You, O Lord, that I may find favor in Your sight, for this favor of *Your grace is sufficient for me* (2 Cor 12:19), even though I lack those gifts which nature desires. I will have nothing to fear from trials and tribulations so long as Your grace is with me. It is my strength, my counsel and my help, more powerful than all my enemies, and wiser than all the worldly-wise.

6. Your grace is the teacher of truth, the master of discipline; it brings light to the heart and solace in affliction; it banishes sorrow, dispels fear, nourishes our devotion and moves us to tears of repentance. What am I without it but a withered tree, a bit of dry timber to be cast into the fire?

Grant, therefore, O Lord, that Your grace always go before me and be ever at my back, keeping me intent upon good works to be done, through Jesus Christ, Your Son and my Lord. Amen.

CHAPTER 56

That We Must Deny Ourselves and Bear the Cross with Christ

CHRIST: My child, as much as you can abandon your self-love, so much will you be able to enter into Me. As the longing for nothing exterior brings you peace, so does the complete surrender of your inmost self unite you with God.

You must learn perfect renunciation of your will to Mine, without contradiction or complaint. Follow Me: *I am the Way, and the Truth, and the Life* (Jn 14:6). Without the way, no human being can go; without the truth, no human being can know; and without life, no human being can live. I am the way you must follow, the truth you must believe, the life you must hope for.

I am the way secure from danger, the truth that cannot deceive, and the life that will never end. I am the straightest way, the supreme truth, the genuine life, the blessed life, the uncreated life. If you keep to My way, you will know the truth and the truth will deliver you, and you will possess everlasting life.

2. *But if you wish to enter into life, keep the commandments* (Mt 19:17); if you want to know the truth, believe Me. *If you wish to be perfect, go, sell your possessions* (Mt 19:21). If you want to be My disciple, deny yourself.

If the possession of eternal bliss is your aim, you must despise this present life. If you want to be exalted in heaven, humble yourself on earth.

If you want to reign with Me, bear the cross with Me; for none but the servants of the cross will find the way of blessedness and everlasting life.

3. *Disciple:* Lord Jesus, inasmuch as Your way is narrow and straight and greatly scorned by the world, give me the grace to bear the world's contempt; for *no student is above a teacher, nor a servant above a master* (Mt 10:24).

Let Your servant meditate on Your life, for there is my salvation and sanctification. Anything else that I read or hear cannot feed my soul or give me full delight.

4. *Christ:* My child, since you know these things and have read about them, you will be blessed if you put them into practice. *Anyone who has received My commandments and observes them is the one who loves Me. . . . I will love and reveal Myself to such a one* (Jn 14:21); and I will make that person sit down with Me in the kingdom of My Father.

5. *Disciple:* Lord Jesus, grant that what You have said and promised may come true for me and may it be my destiny to earn it. I have received the cross from Your hand; I will bear it even unto death, as You have laid it upon me.

The life of any dedicated person is truly a cross, but it is also the way that leads such a person to heaven. We have begun, we may not turn back upon it, and we must never abandon it.

6. Let us, then, all take courage and go forward together; for Jesus indeed is with us. It is for His sake that we have taken this cross upon us,

and it is for His sake that we will persevere to the end. He will help us, for He has gone the way before us.

See, how our King marches before us, and He will fight for us. Let us follow Him courageously, fearing no perils. Let us be ready to die for Him in battle; and let us not stain our honor by abandoning the way of the cross.

CHAPTER 57

That People Should Not Become Dejected When They Fall into Some Defects

CHRIST: I am more pleased, My child, when you are patient and humble under adversity than when you feel devout and consoled in prosperity. Why are you so upset when someone says an unkind word about you?

It could have been worse, but even so, you should not let it disturb you. Forget about it; it is not the first, or anything new; and it will not be the last, if you live long enough.

You are so courageous as long as no opposition comes your way. You also can give good advice and can encourage others with your words; but when some unexpected trouble turns up on your own doorstep, your good advice and moral support fail you.

Think over your great frailty which you often experience in such trifling difficulties. Yet it is for your spiritual help that these and similar things are permitted to happen to you.

RECOURSE TO JESUS IN TIME OF TRIAL—In danger of being swamped by the storm, the disciples implored Jesus: " 'Lord, save us!' . . . Then He stood up and rebuked the winds and the sea, and a great calm ensued" (Mt 8:25f).

2. Resolve in your heart to do the best you can. Then when trials come your way, do not be downcast and do not go over and over them in your heart. If you cannot manage a smile, at least bear them with patience.

Moreover, even though you feel indignant in your heart, control yourself and do not permit any inordinate word to escape your lips lest you scandalize the weak. In this way your indignation will soon calm down and grace will soon return to soothe your hurt feelings.

I still live and am always ready to help and comfort you even more than before, if you will only fully trust Me and devoutly call upon Me.

3. Keep yourself calm and even prepare yourself to undergo greater suffering. All is not lost just because you find yourself often in trouble and grievously tempted. Remember, you are human and not God; you are flesh and blood and not an Angel.

Do you think you can continue in the same state of virtue when this was not found in the Angels in heaven nor in the first man in Eden? I am He Who raises up and supports those who mourn, even lifting up to My Godhead those who know their own weakness.

4. *Disciple:* Blessed be Your holy word, O Lord; for it is sweeter to my mouth than honey and the honeycomb. What would I do in my troubles and anguish if You did not encourage me with Your holy words? What does it matter

what or how much I go through here as long as I reach the haven of salvation at last?

Grant me a happy death, dear Lord, and let my passage out of this world be a peaceful one. Be ever mindful of me, O my God, and direct me in the right path to Your kingdom. Amen.

CHAPTER 58

That People Should Not Search into the Unfathomable Judgments of God

C*HRIST:* My child, you must beware of disputing about matters above your understanding, or about the hidden judgments of God. Do not wonder why one man is forsaken by God, while another receives an abundance of His grace; why this person has so much trouble and the other is so greatly advanced.

These things surpass our comprehension and no mere human discourse can explain the divine judgments. Therefore, when the devil suggests questions to you, or curious people inquire about them, simply reply in the words of the Prophet: *You are righteous, O Lord, and Your judgments are right* (Ps 119:137). Or you can say: *The ordinances of the Lord are true, and all of them are just* (Ps 19:10). My judgments are to be feared, for they are beyond the scope of human reason.

2. Furthermore, there must be no inquiring or disputing concerning the merits of the Saints— which of them is holier than another, or which of them is higher in heaven.

Such discussions are futile; and more often cause dissensions and breed pride and vainglory—with one person trying to exalt a favorite Saint, while someone else argues in favor of another. It accomplishes nothing to try to search into such matters, but it certainly displeases the Saints; *for God is not a God of disorder but of peace* (1 Cor 14:33), and this peace consists in genuine humility, not in self-examination.

3. Some people are attracted to a particular Saint by a kind of emotional devotion rather than a spiritual one. Did I not make all the Saints? And besides, I gave them grace and glory. I know each one's merits; for I preserved them by the blessing of My gracious kindness.

Before all ages I knew My beloved ones; for it was I who chose them, not they who chose Me. They were called by My grace, and through My mercy they were drawn to Me. I led them through many temptations, sustaining them by abundant consolations. I gave them perseverance to the end, and then I crowned their patience.

4. I know them all the first and the last, and I love them with a love beyond all telling. I am to be praised above all My Saints and I am to be blessed and honored in each. Is it not I Who have so gloriously magnified them and, without any previous merit of theirs, bestowed on them the glory they now have?

Therefore, anyone who belittles any of the least of My Saints dishonors also the greatest; for

I have made both the little and the great. And whoever is lacking in respect for any of the Saints is lacking in respect for Me and all others in the kingdom of heaven. They are all one in the bond of perfect charity; having the same thoughts, the same will, and all loving each other as one.

5. But higher than this, they love Me far more than themselves and their own merits. Raised above themselves and drawn away from self-love, they are completely absorbed in the love of Me, in Whom they enjoy their rest. No more can they be turned away or become depressed, for they possess eternal truth and are on fire with an unquenchable charity.

Therefore, let the carnal and worldly-minded, who know nothing of love but self-gratification, stop disputing the state of the Saints according to their own preference instead of according to the eternal truth of God.

6. With many people this is plain ignorance, for, being little enlightened in spiritual matters, they seldom know how to love anyone with a purely spiritual affection. They tend to look upon the things of heaven in the same way as they regard things here on earth, and so they are inclined in their affection for the Saints according to the natural affection of human friendship.

But how vast is the distance between what the imperfect imagine and that which those conceive who are enlightened by divine revelation.

7. Therefore, My child, be careful of curiosity concerning matters beyond your understanding. Your principal occupation and aim should be that you may be found—even though you be the least—in the kingdom of God.

Suppose any persons did learn what Saints were holier, or considered greater in the kingdom of heaven, how would this knowledge benefit them, unless by it they would become more humble in My sight and rise to greater glory to My Name?

Those who think of the greatness of their own sins and the littleness of their virtues, and how far away they are from the perfection of the Saints, are much more pleasing to God than those who argue over which of the Saints is greater or lesser.

It is better to implore the intercession of the Saints by devout prayers and tears and with a humble heart, than by foolish curiosity to inquire into their secrets.

8. The Saints are perfectly contented; if only people would be contented and restrain their useless discourses. The Saints take no glory in their own merits, but attribute all their goodness to Me; because they know that I have given them all out of My infinite charity.

They are so full of love of the Most Holy Trinity and so overflowing with joy, that nothing is wanting to their glory, nor can any happiness be wanting to them. The higher they are in heaven, the humbler they are in themselves, and therefore the nearer to Me and the more beloved by Me.

This is the meaning of the passage in Holy Scripture: *"They throw down their crowns in front of the throne . . . and worship the One Who lives forever and ever"* (Rev 4:10).

9. Many who do not know whether they themselves will be numbered among the least to come into the heavenly kingdom are the very ones who argue about who is the greatest in God's kingdom. It is a great thing to be even the least in heaven, where all are great; for all who enter there will be called the children of God, and so they shall be.

The least shall be as a thousand, and the sinner of a hundred years shall die. When the disciples asked our Lord who was the greatest in the kingdom of heaven, He answered them: *"Unless you change and become like little children, you will never enter the kingdom of heaven. Whoever humbles himself and becomes like this child is the greatest in the kingdom of heaven"* (Mt 18:3-4).

10. Woe to them who disdain to humble themselves willingly as little children; for the gate of the heavenly kingdom is low, and will not permit them to enter. Woe also to the rich who have their comforts in this world. The poor will enter into the kingdom of God, while the rich stand lamenting outside.

So rejoice, you who are humble and poor in spirit. It is to you that the kingdom of God belongs—provided you walk steadfastly in the way of truth.

CHAPTER 59

That All Our Hope and Confidence Is to Be Placed in God Alone

DISCIPLE: My Lord, God, what can I depend on in this life, or what is my greatest solace on earth? Is it not You, my God, Whose mercy is infinite? Where have things gone well with me without You, and where have things gone badly for me when You were with me?

Poverty for Your sake is preferable to riches without You. It would be better to roam this world as a pilgrim with You than to be in heaven without You; for, indeed, where You are not is both death and hell. Heaven is where You are, and You are all I desire, and this desire makes me cry out to You, and in prayer to beg for Your help.

And so I come to the realization that I cannot fully trust in anyone to help me in my necessities save only You—my hope, my trust, my comfort, and my most faithful Friend.

2. *All persons look out for their own interests* (Phil 2:21); You seek only my salvation and my benefit, turning all good things to my good. Even though You permit me to be tested by various temptations and all sorts of trials, You do so for my profit.

It is Your wisdom which deals thus with those whom You love. And under this probation I ought to love and praise You as much as if You were filling me with heavenly consolations.

3. Therefore, in You, O my God, I place all my hope and fly to You for refuge. On You I cast

all my troubles and anxieties; for all is uncertainty, weakness and instability outside of You.

Many friends cannot help me; influential people are of no avail; consulting the wise will not give me the answers I require; the books of the learned can bring me no inspiration; nor is there any precious substance to ransom me, no secret hiding place to shelter me. Only You Yourself, my God, can stand by me, help me, comfort, counsel, teach and defend me.

4. Everything that seems to be for our peace and happiness in this world is really nothing and contributes nothing to our joy, if You are absent. You, Lord, are the end of all good things, the sublimity of life, the depth of all wisdom that can be spoken. Therefore, to trust in You above all else is the greatest comfort Your servants can have.

To You, O Lord, the Father of mercy, I raise my eyes, and in You alone, my God, I put my trust. Bless and sanctify my soul with Your heavenly benediction; may it become a holy place where You may dwell—the place of Your eternal glory. Let nothing be found in this temple that may offend the eyes of Your Divine Majesty.

Look down upon Your poor servant, Lord, exiled in the land of the shadow of death, and according to the greatness of Your goodness and Your manifold mercies, graciously hear my prayer. Defend and preserve my soul amid the many dangers of this corruptible life, and direct me by Your grace along the path of peace, to the land of everlasting light. Amen.

JESUS THE BREAD OF LIFE—"Whoever eats My Flesh and drinks My Blood dwells in Me, and I dwell in him. . . . This is the Bread that came down from heaven. . . . the one who eats this Bread will live forever" (Jn 6:56ff).

BOOK 4

ON THE BLESSED SACRAMENT AND DEVOUT EXHORTATIONS FOR HOLY COMMUNION

THE VOICE OF CHRIST

Come to Me, all you who are weary and overburdened, and I will give you rest (Mt 11:28).

The bread that I will give is My Flesh, for the life of the world (Jn 6:51).

Take this and eat (Mt 26:26). *This is My Body that is for you. Do this in remembrance of Me* (1 Cor 11:24).

Whoever eats My Flesh and drinks My Blood dwells in Me, and I dwell in him (Jn 6:56).

The words I have spoken to you are spirit and life (Jn 6:63).

CHAPTER 1

The Great Reverence with Which Christ Should Be Received

D*ISCIPLE:* These are Your words, O Christ, Who are Eternal Truth, although they have not all been uttered at the same time, nor written in one same place. Nevertheless, they are Your words, and they express the truth; that is why I receive them all with gratitude and faith.

They are Your words; You have spoken them. But they are also mine because You have given them for my salvation. I eagerly receive them from Your mouth that they may be permanently implanted in my heart.

These words are full of tenderness and gentleness, and they give me courage. But I am terrified by my sins, and my unclean conscience prevents me from coming near so great a mystery. Your loving words invite me, but I am weighed down by my numerous offenses.

2. You tell me to come to You with confidence, if I desire to have a share in Your life; and to receive the food of immortality, if I want to attain everlasting life and glory. "*Come,*" You say, "*to me, all you who are weary and overburdened, and I will give you rest*" (Mt 11:28).

These words are heartening to the ear of a sinner. To think that You, my Lord and God, actually invite the poor and needy to the Communion of Your Most Sacred Body! But who am I, Lord, to dare approach You? You, Whom the heaven of heavens cannot contain; yet You say to me: "Come to Me, all of you."

3. What is the meaning of this humble compassion and so friendly an invitation? Since I am unaware of any good in myself and have so often grievously offended You, how can I receive You under my roof? Why, the very Angels and Archangels stand in awe of You; the Saints and

the just tremble; and still You say: "Come to Me, all of you."

Lord, how could I possibly believe this, if You had not said these words? And how could I possibly venture near You, unless You had commanded it?

4. That just man, Noah, toiled for a hundred years to build the ark so that he and a remnant might be saved; how then can I, in just one hour, prepare myself to receive the Creator of the world with due reverence?

Your great servant and special friend, Moses, made an ark of imperishable wood, overlaying it with purest gold, to place the Tables of the Law in it; then how shall I, a corrupt and perishable creature, dare so lightly to receive the Maker of the Law and the Giver of life?

It took seven years for Solomon, the wisest of Israel's kings, to build a resplendent temple for the worship of Your Name, the dedication of which was celebrated for eight days; a thousand peace offerings were sacrificed—and with great solemnity and rejoicing—and accompanied by the sound of trumpets, the Ark of the Covenant was carried in solemn procession to the place prepared for it.

And I, the most miserable and poorest of human beings, who can scarcely spend one devout half-hour, shall I bring You into my house? If only I could spend just one half-hour as I ought!

5. O my God, how much did those great persons of the Old Testament do to please You!

How little I do and how short is the time I give to prepare myself for the reception of Holy Communion! I am neither recollected nor free from distractions.

Certainly, no unworthy thought should arise, nor should my mind be occupied with any created thing. Indeed, it is not an Angel I am about to receive into my heart, but the Lord of the Angels.

6. What a vast difference there is between the Ark of the Covenant with its relics, and Your most precious Body with its incomparable virtues. For those sacrifices of the Law prefigured what was to come; while the Sacrifice of Your Body is the fulfillment of those ancient sacrifices.

7. Why, then, do I not seek Your adorable Presence with ardent longing? And why do I not prepare myself with meticulous care to receive this most holy Sacrament, since the ancient Patriarchs and Prophets, kings and princes, too, together with all the people, displayed such affectionate devotion for divine worship?

8. King David, that most devout ruler, danced before the Ark of the Covenant with all his might when he remembered all the favors bestowed on his forefathers. He made various kinds of musical instruments and composed psalms.

These he ordered to be sung joyfully by all the people; and he also sang them himself to the accompaniment of his harp, when inspired by the grace of the Holy Spirit. He taught and exhorted the people to praise God with all their heart, blessing Him in unison every day.

If the people of ancient times showed such reverence and devotion to God in the presence of the Ark of the Covenant, how much greater should be the reverence and devotion to Your presence in the Blessed Sacrament paid by me and all Christian people, as also in the receiving of the precious Body and Blood of our Lord, Jesus Christ.

9. Many people travel great distances to visit the relics of Saints and marvel on hearing of their remarkable deeds. They gaze upon magnificent churches dedicated to them, paying homage to their blessed remains, wrapped with silk and covered with gold.

But You, my God, the Saint of Saints, Creator of all things, and Lord of Angels, are here present on the altar before me! People are often excited by curiosity and novel sights, and so they return with little inclination toward amendment of life, especially when their pilgrimages are made hurriedly, going from one place to another, and no thought is given to true contrition for their sins.

In the Sacrament of the altar, You are wholly present, God and Man; and here also, in all its abundance, is the fruit of eternal salvation, as often as You are received worthily and devoutly. To this Sacrament we are drawn not by curiosity, levity, or sensuality, but only by firm faith, devout hope, and pure charity.

10. O God, the invisible Creator of all the world, how wonderful are Your ways with us!

How kind and gracious are Your dealings with Your chosen ones, to whom You offer Yourself to be received in this most holy Sacrament!

It far surpasses all understanding, drawing the hearts of the devout in a special manner and enkindling their love. Your faithful ones, who give all their lives to amendment, often receive from this adorable Sacrament the grace of devotion and the love of virtue.

11. Wonderful and hidden is the grace bestowed by this Sacrament on the faithful of Christ, which unbelievers and those who give their lives up to sin can never experience! For spiritual grace is conferred by this Sacrament, lost virtue is renewed in the soul, and the beauty destroyed by sin returns again.

Sometimes the grace of this Sacrament is so powerful, that from the fullness of devotion granted, not only the mind, but also the frail body recovers its former strength.

12. What a pity, and how much we ought to regret that we are so lukewarm and careless, as not to be drawn with greater love to receive Christ, our Lord; for in Him is all the hope and merit of those who are to be saved. He is our sanctification and redemption; the comforter of pilgrims, and the eternal joy of the Saints.

Therefore, it is most regrettable that many have so little regard for this saving mystery, which fills heaven with joy and keeps all the world in being. How blind and hard are human hearts, when they pay such scant attention to so wonderful a gift, that even their daily reception of Holy Communion falls into mere routine!

13. If this most holy Sacrament were celebrated in one place only, and consecrated by only one priest in all the world, think how great would be the longing of people's hearts, and how they would flock to that place and visit that one priest of God in order to see the divine mysteries celebrated!

But now there are many priests, and in many places Christ is offered up, so that as Holy Communion is more widely distributed throughout the world, the greater appears God's grace and love for human beings.

Thank You, Lord Jesus, eternal Shepherd, that You have graciously fulfilled Your promise to feed Your poor exiles with Your precious Body and Blood, inviting us to receive these sacred mysteries with the words from Your own lips, saying: *"Come to Me, all you who are weary and overburdened, and I will give you rest"* (Mt 11:28).

CHAPTER 2

On the Great Goodness of God Shown Human Beings in the Blessed Sacrament

DISCIPLE: O Lord Jesus, trusting in Your infinite goodness and mercy, I come to my Divine Physician in my sickness, to the Fountain of life in my hunger and thirst, to the King of heaven in my great need, to my Lord as a servant, to my Creator as a creature, and to my living Consoler in my desolation.

But who am I that You should come to me? Who am I that You should give Yourself to me? How dare I, a wretched sinner, approach You? And how do You, in Your greatness, come to such a sinner? You know Your servant and know that of myself I have no goodness in me to deserve such a favor from You.

Therefore, I confess my unworthiness and acknowledge Your overwhelming kindness; I praise Your mercy and I thank You for Your limitless love. You do this, not because of any merit on my part, but for Your own sake, that Your goodness may be more apparent to me, Your love more abundantly bestowed, and Your humility more perfectly manifested.

Since, then, this pleases You and You have willed it so, this graciousness of Yours also pleases me; and I pray that my iniquity may not resist it.

2. O sweetest and kindest Jesus, how great must be the reverence, the thanks and unending praise shown to You for this great gift of receiving Your sacred Body, whose dignity no human can express in words! What should be my disposition as I approach You, my Lord, in this holy Communion—You, Whom I long to receive devoutly, yet can never venerate sufficiently?

What better thought can I have for my soul's profit than to humble myself completely in Your presence, forever praising Your infinite goodness to me? May You be praised and glorified forever, my God; while I despise myself to the depths of my nothingness and cast myself at Your feet.

3. You are the Saint of all Saints, Lord, while I am the lowest of sinners. You bow Yourself down to me, who am unable and unworthy to look up to You. You come to me, desiring to be with me and to invite me to Your feast.

You desire to give me heavenly food to eat—even the *Bread of Angels* (Ps 78:25); none other than Yourself, the living Bread, Who came down from heaven and gives life to the world.

4. Behold, where love has its source and what lowliness shines upon us! How great ought to be our praise and thanksgiving to You for such a gift! Your plan in instituting this Sacrament was truly for the health and welfare of our souls— truly a joyous feast in which You give Yourself to be our food.

How marvelous is Your work, dear Lord, and how mighty Your power! Your truth is infallible! You spoke, and all things came into being as You commanded.

5. What a wonderful thing, deserving of all faith—far above human understanding—that You, my Lord and my God, true God and true Man, are wholly contained beneath the form of bread and wine, eaten yet not consumed, by whoever receives You. You, the Lord of all things, dependent upon no one, would dwell in us by means of this Sacrament.

Keep my heart and my body free from sin, that, with a happy and clean conscience, I may take part in Your sacred mysteries; and may receive what You have instituted for my eternal salvation, for Your own honor and perpetual memorial.

6. Rejoice, my soul, and thank God for such a precious gift, which He has left you for so unique a solace in this valley of tears. Every time you renew this mystery and receive the Body of Christ, you further the work of your redemption and you partake in all the merits of Christ.

Christ's love for us never diminishes, nor is the greatness of His atonement ever consumed. Therefore, by spiritual renewal prepare yourself to receive the Blessed Sacrament, and prayerfully consider the great mystery of redemption.

Whenever you celebrate or hear Mass, it should seem to you as great, as new, and as joyful, as if Christ that same day had first come down into the womb of the Virgin Mary and become Man; or, as if He that same day—hanging on the cross—suffered and died for our salvation.

CHAPTER 3

On the Advantage of Frequent Communion

D*ISCIPLE:* I come to You, O Lord, that I may benefit by Your gift and rejoice in that holy feast, which *in Your goodness,* O my God, *You have provided for the poor* (Ps 68:11). In You is all that I can or should wish for; You are my salvation and my redemption, my hope and my strength, my honor and my glory.

Today, *give joy to the soul of Your servant, for to You, O Lord, I lift up my soul* (Ps 86:4). Now I desire to receive You into my house with devotion and reverence, that, like Zacchaeus, I may deserve to receive Your blessing and to find a place among the children of Abraham. My soul longs for Your Body; my heart desires to be made one with You.

2. Give Yourself to me, Lord, and it is enough, for apart from You there is no consolation. I cannot exist without You, nor can I live if You do not visit me. Therefore, I must come to You frequently, and receive You for the health of my soul. If I do not, I shall surely faint by the wayside, being deprived of this heavenly food.

Most merciful Jesus, when You preached to the people and healed them of their various diseases, You Yourself said, *"I do not want to send them away hungry, or they may collapse on the way"* (Mt 15:32). Please deal with me the same way, You, Who have left Yourself in this Sacrament for the comfort of the faithful.

You are the soul's true nourishment, and the person who receives You worthily will share in the inheritance of everlasting glory. Certainly it is necessary for me—who so often commit sin, so soon grow dull and weary—to renew and cleanse myself by frequent prayers and confessions and by fervently receiving Your Body, so that I may not fall away from my holy resolutions through the neglect of these means.

3. People's senses are prone to evil from their youth, and unless they are strengthened by the divine medicine, they soon fall into greater sins. Therefore, Holy Communion draws people away from evil and strengthens them in goodness. If I am now often careless and lukewarm when I celebrate Mass or receive Communion, what would I be like if I did not take this remedy, nor sought the help it gives me?

Even though I am not prepared nor do I have the proper dispositions to receive my Lord every day, nevertheless, I will see to it that I do receive Him at certain times, that I may share in so great a grace. This is the chief consolation of the faithful soul as long as it remains far from You, imprisoned in this mortal body, that mindful of God, it frequently receives the Beloved with a warm heart.

4. How wonderful are Your ways with us, O Lord, that You take such pity on us and bend to our lowliness! That You, the Creator, Who gives life to all souls, should come to so unworthy a creature to refresh his hunger with Your divinity and humanity.

Happy and blessed are the souls which are in the state to receive You, Lord God, with devotion, and in the reception to be filled with spiritual joy! How great a Lord do they receive, how beloved a Guest do they bring into their houses! What a pleasant Companion, what a faithful Friend! How noble and beautiful a Spouse—to be loved above all other loves and beyond all that can be desired.

O my dearly Beloved, let the heavens and earth, with all their adornment, be silent before You; for whatever beauty or glory they possess is the gift of Your generous goodness, and they can never attain to the beauty of Your Name, You, Whose wisdom is without limit.

CHAPTER 4

On the Many Benefits Bestowed on Those Who Communicate Devoutly

DISCIPLE: O Lord, my God, grant Your servant the blessing of Your kindness, that I may be worthy to approach Your sublime Sacrament with true devotion. Rouse me from the sloth and idleness which have gripped me, that my heart may more readily be lifted up to You.

Come to me with Your saving presence, and let me in spirit taste Your sweetness, which lies hidden in the most Blessed Sacrament as in a plentiful fountain. Give light to my eyes, too, that I may gaze upon this great mystery, and strengthen me to believe it with persevering faith.

It is You Who effect this work; no human being has such power. It is Your holy institution and not human invention. No human beings are able to grasp and understand these things of themselves, for they are far above even the keen intelligence of the Angels. And shall I, a wretched sinner, mere dust and ashes, be able to probe and grasp so sacred and incomprehensible a mystery?

2. Dear Lord, with simplicity of heart, in good and stable faith, and at Your command, I approach You—full of confidence and adoration—truly believing that You are present in this Sacrament, God and Man. It is Your will that I receive You and bind myself to You in love.

Most merciful Lord, I beg of You that special grace, that my soul may melt and overflow with Your love, never concerning myself again with any other comfort but Your own. This most exalted and worthy Sacrament is the health of both soul and body, the remedy for every spiritual sickness.

By it all vices are cured, passions restrained, temptations overcome or diminished; by it grace is poured forth, confirming faith, strengthening hope, inflaming and enlarging charity.

3. O my God, the support of my soul, the repairer of human infirmity, and the giver of all spiritual consolation, You have given—and frequently still give—many blessings in this Sacrament to those beloved souls who receive You with devotion.

Many are the comforts You give them to sustain them in all their troubles; from the depths of their own misery You lift them up, giving Your elect the hope of Your protection. You renew them and enlighten them interiorly—and with a kind of new grace—so that those who felt anxiety and abandoned without love before Communion were changed for the better after receiving this heavenly food and drink.

You are pleased to deal with Your chosen ones in this way, that they may more fully realize and admit their own weakness; and how much they gain in goodness and grace from You. Of themselves they are cold, dry and lacking in devotion; but after receiving You, they become fervent, cheerful and devout.

Who can come humbly to the fountain of sweetness without carrying away with them some of its sweetness? Or who can stand by a blazing fire and not feel some of its heat? You, O Lord, are a fountain, ever full and overflowing, a fire always burning and never dying out.

4. Therefore, although I may not draw from the fullness of this fountain, nor drink till my thirst is quenched, I will at least sip a few drops of these heavenly waters, that I may not be utterly parched.

If I cannot be entirely spiritual and, like the Cherubim and Seraphim, be on fire with charity, I will try at least to be sincere in my devotion and to prepare my heart, so that through the humble reception of this life-giving Sacrament, I may catch some small spark of the divine fire.

O Jesus, my holy Savior, from Your gracious kindness, supply what is wanting in me, for You did not refuse to call all to Yourself, saying: *"Come to Me, all you who are weary and overburdened, and I will give you rest"* (Mt 11:28).

5. I labor, indeed, in the sweat of my brow; I am tormented by a sorrowful heart, burdened by my sins, troubled with temptations, and caught up in and oppressed by many evil passions, but there is no one to help me. For who can deliver me and save me, and to whom can I commit myself and all that is mine, except You, Lord God, my Savior?

You, Who have prepared Your Body and Blood for my food and drink, save me, receive me, for the praise and glory of Your Name, and bring me to everlasting life. Grant me, O Lord, my Savior, a daily increase in devotion, through the frequent reception of Your sacred mystery.

CHAPTER 5

On the Dignity of the Sacrament and on the Priestly Office

CHRIST: If you had the purity of an Angel and the holiness of St. John the Baptist, you would not be worthy to receive or to touch this holy Sacrament. No human being has merited to be able to consecrate and touch the Sacrament of Christ, or to receive the Bread of Angels as food.

This is a tremendous mystery, and great is the dignity conferred on priests, which is not granted to the Angels. For only priests, validly ordained in the Church, have this power of offering Holy Mass and consecrating the Body of Christ.

The priest stands in the place of Christ, using God's word according to His command and institution; but God Himself is the principal Author and unseen Worker in this Sacrament. To Him is subject all that He wills to be, and everything obeys His command.

Therefore, you should believe Almighty God more concerning this most wonderful Sacrament than what your own senses or any visible sign indicates. With what fear and reverence are you to approach this holy work! Look to yourself, and consider the Source of this ministry that was delivered to you by the imposition of the Bishop's hands.

Now you have been made a priest, consecrated to offer Mass. See to it that you offer this adorable Sacrifice to God with great reverence and devotion, and that the life you lead be blameless. You have not lightened your burden; but, on the contrary, you are bound by a stricter self-discipline and are obliged to strive for higher perfection.

Your obligation requires you to be adorned with all virtues in order to give others the example of a good life. A priest's conversation must not be on the level of the crude ways of the world, but rather with the Angels in heaven, or with holy people of perfect life on earth.

2. A priest clothed in his sacred vestments takes the place of Christ, offering humble prayer and supplication to God for himself and for all his people. Before him and behind him he wears

the cross of our Lord, that he may always be mindful of the Passion of Christ.

He bears the cross before him that he may earnestly behold the footsteps of Christ and strive fervently to follow them; he bears the cross behind him that he may humbly suffer for God whatever injuries are done to him by others. Again, he wears the cross before him that he may have sorrow for his own sins; and behind him that he may realize that he has been placed between God and humankind in order to mourn over the sins of others with compassion.

He ought not to grow weary of prayer and offering the Holy Sacrifice until he merits to obtain grace and mercy. When a priest offers Mass, he honors God, gives joy to the Angels, builds up the Church, helps the living and obtains rest for the departed, making himself a sharer of all good things.

CHAPTER 6

On the Question of Proper Preparation before Communion

DISCIPLE: I am very fearful, O Lord, and inwardly confused, when I think of Your greatness and my own wretchedness; because if I fail to receive You, I run away from life; and if I receive You unworthily, I incur Your wrath. What, then, must I do, O my God, my helper and consoler in all necessities?

2. Please teach me the right way; inspire me with some short exercise suitable for Holy Communion. For it is necessary for me to know how I ought to prepare my heart to receive You with reverence and devotion for the good of my soul, or to offer so great and divine a sacrifice.

CHAPTER 7

On the Examination of Our Conscience and on the Firm Purpose of Amendment

CHRIST: Above all things, the priest of God should come to offer, handle and receive this Sacrament with great humility and reverence of heart, full of faith and the loving intention of giving honor to God. Examine your conscience carefully and, to the best of your ability, cleanse and purify it by sincere contrition and a humble confession, so that you may not be aware of anything to fill you with remorse, or prevent your free approach to God.

Be sorry for all your sins in general, and especially regret and have sorrow for your daily offenses. If time permits, tell God—in the secrecy of your heart—all the miseries caused by your unruly passions.

2. Be full of grief and lament that you are still attached to the flesh and the world, so unmortified in your passions; so full of unsuppressed evil desires, so unguarded in your outward senses, so often engaged in useless imaginings; so readily

drawn to things outside, so neglectful of those within.

Bewail the fact that you are so easily moved to laughter and frivolity, so slow to weep and repent; so inclined to relaxation and bodily comforts, so slothful in austerity and fervor of spirit; so eager for news and to see nice things, so reluctant to welcome humiliation and contempt; so craving for possessions, so stingy in giving and so obstinate in retaining.

Grieve that you are so thoughtless in speech, so undisciplined in silence; so unmannerly in habit, so inconsiderate in action; so greedy for food, so deaf to the word of God; so quick to rest, so slow to work; so alert to gossip, so drowsy at holy vigils; so hasty to reach the end, so wandering in attention; so careless in prayer, so lukewarm at Mass, so lacking in fervor at Communion.

Deplore the fact that you are so soon distracted, so seldom wholly recollected; so suddenly moved to anger, so ready to take offense at others; so prone to judge, so severe in rebuke; so happy in prosperity, so morose in adversity; so often proposing good resolutions, and so rarely fulfilling them.

3. When you have confessed and regretted these and all your faults, being contrite and greatly displeased at your own weakness, firmly resolve to amend your life, and to advance in the life of holiness. Then, with complete abandonment of your will, offer yourself up on the altar of your heart, as an unending sacrifice to the honor of My Name.

Give both your soul and your body into My keeping, that you may be found worthy to offer sacrifice to God and to receive the Sacrament of My Body with profit.

4. There is no more worthy oblation, no greater means to wash away sin, than to offer yourself purely and wholly to God, together with the offering of the Body of Christ in Holy Mass and Communion.

If people do all they can, and are truly sorry for their sins, as often as they come to Me for grace and forgiveness, I am the Lord God, Who says: *Do I take any pleasure in the death of the wicked? . . . Do I not rather rejoice when they turn from their ways and live?* (Ezek 18:23). I will no longer remember their sins, but all will be forgiven them.

CHAPTER 8

On the Offering of Christ on the Cross, and the Resignation of Ourselves

C*HRIST:* With arms outstretched upon the cross, I hung stripped and naked, with nothing remaining in Me which was not turned into a complete sacrifice; I willingly offered Myself to God the Father, to appease the divine wrath and to satisfy for your sins. Should you not willingly, therefore, daily offer yourself to Me in the Mass, with all the strength and the devotion of your heart, as a pure and holy oblation?

I ask nothing more of you than this: your efforts to surrender yourself wholly to Me. I care for nothing else that you can give besides yourself; for it is not your gift but you that I seek.

2. Since it would not satisfy you if you had everything but Me, so neither am I pleased with anything you give if you do not offer Me yourself. Give yourself to Me—your entire self to your God—and your offering will be accepted.

See how I offered Myself wholly to the Father for you; I gave My Body and Blood to be your food, that I might be all yours, and you completely Mine. But if you rely on yourself and will not offer yourself freely to My will, your offering is incomplete, and a perfect union will not exist between us.

Before all else, you must make a willing offering of yourself into God's hands, if you wish to obtain grace and freedom. The reason why so few are inwardly free and enlightened is because so few give themselves completely.

My words are unchanged: *"Anyone of you who does not renounce all of his possessions cannot be My disciple"* (Lk 14:33). Therefore, if you wish to be My disciple, offer up yourself to Me with all your affections.

CHAPTER 9

We Must Offer Ourselves and All That is OUrs to God, and Pray for All People

DISCIPLE: Lord, all things in heaven and on earth are Yours. I desire to give myself to You in willing abandonment, and to remain Yours forever. Lord, in simplicity of heart, I offer myself to You this day, always to be Your obedient servant and a sacrifice of perpetual praise.

Accept me with this holy sacrifice of Your precious Body, which I offer You today in the presence of Your assisting Angels, for my salvation and that of all Your people.

2. Lord, I offer You all my sins and offenses, committed before You and Your holy Angels, from the day I was first able to sin until now. Placing them upon Your altar of reconciliation, I implore You to burn and consume them in the fire of Your love.

Wipe clean from the slate of my conscience every stain of sin and every fault; and restore to me Your grace, which I have lost through sin, granting me full pardon of all, and in Your mercy receiving me with the kiss of peace.

3. What else can I do about my sins but humbly confess and deplore them, ever asking for Your mercy? Please hear me, O merciful God, as I stand before You. All my sins are extremely detestable to me; by Your grace, I will never commit them again.

I am truly sorry for them and will regret them the rest of my life; and I am ready to do penance and make amends to the best of my ability. O my God, I beg You to forgive my sins, for Your holy Name's sake. Be pleased to save my soul, which You have redeemed by Your precious Blood. I commit myself to Your mercy, resigning myself with confidence into Your hands.

4. Although my good works are few and imperfect, nevertheless I offer them to You to improve and sanctify. Look upon them favorably, making them acceptable to You, always perfecting them; and bring me, a slothful and useless creature, to a holy and glorious end.

5. I offer You also all the holy desires of devout persons; the needs of my parents, brothers, sisters, friends, and all who are dear to me; and all who have shown kindness to me or others for Your love, or who have asked me to pray and offer Masses for them and those dear to them—living or dead.

May they be helped by Your grace and consolation, protected from dangers and delivered from their pains. Then, freed from all evils, they may joyfully give You praise and thanks.

6. I offer You as well my prayers and this sacrifice of reconciliation especially for those who hurt me, offended me, abused me, or inflicted any injury upon me; and for all, too, whom I have at any time burdened, grieved, troubled or prevented from good—by word or deed, knowingly or unknowingly.

Be pleased to forgive us all our sins and mutual offenses. Drive from our hearts, O Lord, all suspicion, perversity, anger, dissension, and whatever else may wound charity or lessen brotherly love. Be merciful, O Lord, be merciful to those who implore Your mercy; give grace to those in need; make us all live in such a way as to be worthy to possess Your grace and life everlasting. Amen.

CHAPTER 10

That We Must Not Lightly Refrain from Holy Communion

CHRIST: Frequently go to the fountain of grace and divine mercy—the fountain of goodness and all purity—where you can be cured of your passions and vices. Then you may deserve to be made stronger and more watchful in resisting all the temptations and deceits of Satan.

This enemy is aware of the great benefit and remedy for sin contained in Holy Communion, and tries by every ruse and occasion he can to withdraw and prevent faithful souls from it.

2. Therefore, some people experience the worst attacks and deceits of this fiend when they are preparing to receive Holy Communion. As Job tells us: the evil spirit comes among the children of God, to disturb them with his usual malice, or to frighten and confuse them, so that he may, through his crafty suggestions, lessen their devotion or destroy their faith; this is to

make them either abandon Communion, or approach with little fervor.

You must completely ignore his wiles—however foul and abominable; turn all his filthy suggestions back upon him. Satan must be treated with utter scorn and contempt. Never refrain from Holy Communion because of his attacks and the disturbances he arouses.

3. Often a person is overanxious to have a feeling of devotion, or has some concern about going to confession, which creates an obstacle. Follow the advice of the wise and dismiss all anxiety or scruple, for this hinders the grace of God and destroys devotion of mind.

Do not give up going to Holy Communion for every little disturbance; but go promptly to confession, and freely forgive others any offenses against you. If you are the offender, humbly ask pardon, and God will freely forgive you.

4. What good does it do you to delay your confession or put off going to Holy Communion? The sooner you cleanse yourself, spit out the poison and take the remedy, the sooner you will feel better than if you had delayed doing so. If for any reason you do not receive it today, tomorrow some worse thing may befall you; and so you may be kept from Communion a long time, meanwhile becoming more unfit to receive it.

Shake off your apathy as soon as you can, for it will do you no good to continue in a state of distress and uncertainty, and because of these to keep away from the sacraments. Indeed, it is very harmful to delay receiving Communion for long, for this usually results in spiritual inertia.

Sad to say, there are people lacking in devotion and self-discipline, who easily find excuses for delaying their confession, and so they put off their Communion too, for fear they will have to keep a greater watch over themselves.

5. How little love and what weak devotion do they have who so easily neglect Holy Communion! How happy and how acceptable to God are those persons who live such a life and keep such guard over their consciences that they are prepared to receive Holy Communion every day.

They are to be praised for their reverence if, through humility or for some lawful reason, they refrain from going to Communion. But if laziness has taken hold of them, then they must rouse themselves and do their best; and the Lord will come to help them in their desire because of their goodwill, for which He has high regard.

6. When people are prevented legitimately from receiving Holy Communion, if they still keep their good and pious intention to do so, they will not be deprived of the blessings it brings them. Every devout person may make a spiritual Communion with our Lord—every day and every hour—without any prohibition, and will profit greatly from this.

But on certain days and at definite times, you should receive the Body of your Redeemer sacramentally, with loving reverence and for the praise and honor of God rather than for your own consolation. As often as you communicate mystically and devoutly recall the mystery of Christ's Incarnation and Passion, your heart will be inflamed with the fire of His love.

But those who only prepare themselves when a feast day occurs, or when custom dictates, will most often find themselves unprepared. They are truly blessed who, every time they offer Mass or receive Communion, offer themselves entirely to our Lord.

In celebrating Holy Mass, be neither too slow nor too hurried, but maintain the good medium way of those with whom you live. You ought not to do what would burden or weary others; but keep to the ways prescribed by the holy Fathers, conforming yourself to what will profit other people rather than your personal liking or devotion.

CHAPTER 11

The Body of Christ and Holy Scripture Are Most Necessary to the Faithful Soul

D*ISCIPLE:* O Lord Jesus, how great is the sweetness of the devout soul fed by You at Your heavenly banquet, where there is no other but Yourself—the soul's only Beloved—the One to be desired above all the desires of the heart! What a delight it would be for me if I could weep before You, with deep and humble love, washing Your feet with my tears as did the devoted Mary Magdalene.

But where is this devotion, and where the abundant outpouring of holy tears? Certainly my heart should be on fire and weep for joy here before You and Your holy Angels, for You are really present with me in this sacred Sacrament, though hidden beneath another form.

2. My eyes could not stand to look upon You in Your real divine glory, nor could the whole world bear to see You in the splendor of Your majesty. But You consider my weakness and conceal Yourself beneath this Sacrament. I truly possess and adore by faith Him Whom the Angels adore unveiled in heaven.

I must be content to possess and to walk in the light of true faith, until the day of everlasting glory breaks upon me and the shadows of figures shall pass away. But *when we encounter what is perfect* (1 Cor 13:10), there will be no need for sacraments; for the Blessed in heaven have no need of the healing aid of the sacraments.

Their joy is without end, as in His presence they gaze upon the glory of God, face to face. Transformed from their own brightness into the glory of the infinite God, they taste the Word of God made Man, as He was from the beginning and will be forever.

3. When I recall all these wonders, even spiritual comforts become burdensome to me; for as long as I do not see my Lord in all His glory, nothing that I see and hear in this world means anything to me. O my God, You are my witness that nothing can comfort me, nor any creature

bring me rest, but only You, my God, Whom I long to see for all eternity.

But this is impossible as long as I remain in this mortal life. Therefore, I must determine to be very patient and to submit myself to You in all my desires.

Your Saints—who now rejoice with You in the kingdom of heaven, O Lord—during their lifetime had to wait in faith and much patience for the coming of Your glory. What they believed, I believe; what they hoped for, I hope for; and where they have arrived, I trust that through Your grace, I too shall arrive.

Until then, 1 will walk in faith, strengthened by the examples of Your Saints. I also will have the Holy Scriptures to comfort me and to be a mirror of the life I must lead; above all these I will have Your most holy Body for my special remedy and refuge.

4. In this life there are two things I particularly need, without which this miserable life would be unbearable. While detained in the prison of my body, I confess my need for two things: food and light. Knowing my weakness, You have given me Your holy Body for the nourishment of my soul and body, and *Your word as a lamp for my feet* (Ps 119:105).

Without these two I cannot live well; for the word of God is the light of my soul, and Your Sacrament is the Bread of life. These may be called the two tables set on either side in the treasury of holy Church.

One is the table of the holy altar, having on it the holy bread—the precious Body of Christ; the other is that of the divine law, containing holy doctrine, instructing us in the true faith and leading us securely even beyond the inner veil wherein is the Holy of Holies.

5. O Lord Jesus, Eternal Light, I thank You for this table of holy doctrine, which You have set before us by the ministry of Your servants, the Prophets and Apostles, and other holy teachers. O Creator and Redeemer of human beings, I thank You also for showing the whole world Your love by preparing a great feast.

You have not set before us the lamb of the Old Law, but Your most sacred Body and Blood, rejoicing the hearts of all faithful people with Your holy Banquet and giving them the cup of salvation to drink, in which are all the delights of heaven. The holy Angels also feast with us, but with a joy greater than ours.

6. How great and honorable is the office of priests, who have been empowered to consecrate with sacred words the Lord of all majesty, to bless Him with their lips, to hold Him in their hands, to receive Him with their mouth, and to administer Him to others!

How clean should be the hands, how pure the mouth, how holy the body, and how undefiled the heart of the priest, into whom the Author of all purity so often enters. Therefore, from the mouth of a priest, who so frequently receives the Sacrament of Christ, no word but what is holy, truthful and beneficial to others should come forth.

7. His eyes, accustomed to looking upon the Body of Christ, should be simple and chaste; his hands, which touch the Creator of heaven and earth, pure and lifted up to heaven. To priests in particular are addressed those words in the Law: *Be holy, for I am holy. I am the Lord your God* (Lev 19:2).

8. O Almighty God, help them by Your grace, that they who have received the office of the priesthood may serve You worthily and devoutly in all purity and with a good conscience.

And if they cannot live in as great innocence as they ought, grant them at least the grace to mourn the sins they have committed, so that in the spirit of humility and the resolution of a good will, they may serve You in the future with greater fervor.

CHAPTER 12

On How We Should Prepare to Receive Christ in Holy Communion

CHRIST: I am the Lover of purity and Giver of all holiness. I seek a pure heart and there I make My resting place. Make ready for Me a large upper room, furnished, and there with My disciples I will eat the Pasch with you. If you want Me to come to you and to remain with you, rid yourselves of the old leaven and cleanse the dwelling place of your heart.

Shut out the whole world and the clamor of evil passions; sit like a lone sparrow on the housetop, thinking over your sins in the bitterness of your soul. For every lover prepares the best and most beautiful place for the dearly beloved, since this is how the one who entertains the beloved shows affectionate welcome.

2. Nevertheless, you must realize that you cannot make adequate preparation for Me through your own merits, even if you prepared yourself for an entire year and with your mind on nothing else. It is through My generosity and grace that you are allowed to approach My table; just as if a beggar were invited to a rich man's dinner and could only return him thanks for the kindness shown to him.

Do the best you can and as well as you can; not from habit or necessity, but with reverential fear and affection, receive the Body of your beloved Lord God, Who condescends to come to you. I am He Who has invited you, and I have commanded this Sacrament to be; therefore, I will make up for whatever is lacking in you. Come, then, and receive Me.

3. When I give the grace of devotion to you, thank your God—not because you are worthy, but because I have taken pity on you. If you find yourself dry, with no devotion, persevere in prayer, sigh and knock at My door; and do not

stop until you receive some crumb or drop of this saving grace.

You need Me; I have no need of you. It is not you who come to make Me holy, but I come to sanctify you and make you better than you were before.

You come in order to be sanctified and united to Me, that you may receive new grace and, incited anew, amend your life. Do not neglect this grace, but carefully prepare your heart and then bring into it your Beloved.

4. But it is not enough to prepare yourself by devotion before Communion; also you should keep yourself in a devout frame of mind after receiving this Sacrament. It is just as necessary to be watchful after as is the devout preparation beforehand; for careful guarding of devotion afterward is the best preparation for obtaining new grace.

You will not be well disposed to receive this new grace if you immediately turn aside to worldly pleasures. Beware of much speaking; remain recollected with your God; for you have Him within you Whom all the world cannot take from you. I am He to Whom you should give your whole being; so that henceforth—free from all care—you may no longer live for yourself but for Me.

CHAPTER 13

A Devout Soul Should Long with the Whole Heart to Be United to Christ in the Blessed Sacrament

DISCIPLE: If only I could find You alone, O Lord, and tell You all that is in my heart! Then I could enjoy You as much as my soul desires; then no one would disregard me, nor anything created concern or bother me; then You only would speak to me and I to You, as a lover does to a beloved, or a friend to a good friend.

This is my one desire and what I pray for: to be entirely united to You, and to withdraw my heart from all created things, that by Holy Communion and the frequent offering of Mass, I may learn ever to delight in the eternal things of heaven.

Dear Lord, when shall I be completely one with You and entirely forgetful of myself? You in me and I in You; grant that we may be always so and remain as one forever.

2. You are truly my Beloved. "Among ten thousand you shall know Him"; in You my soul delights to dwell all the days of my life. In You, the Lord of peace, is my supreme peace and real rest; and without You is only toil, sorrow and endless misery.

Truly You are a hidden God (Isa 45:15), and You have nothing to do with evil people, but You speak with the humble and simple of heart. How sweet is Your Spirit, O Lord, Who consents to refresh Your children with that most delicious

Bread which comes down from heaven in order to show them Your loving kindness!

For what other great nation is there that has gods so near to it (Deut 4:7) as You, our God, are to all Your faithful ones, to whom You give Yourself as food and drink for their daily refreshment, and to raise their hearts to heaven!

3. What other people is so fortunate as the Christian people? What creature under heaven is so beloved as a devout soul into whom God comes, in order to feed him with His own glorious Body and Blood? O grace unspeakable, O marvelous condescension, O love without measure, bestowed only on human beings!

There is nothing I can give to the Lord for this grace—this supreme love; nothing acceptable I can offer Him but my heart entirely given to God and closely united to Him. Then, all that is within me will be filled with joy when my soul is perfectly one with God.

Then He will say to me: "If you will be with Me, I will be with you." And I will answer Him and say: "Stay with me, Lord, I implore You; for my desire is to be with You." This is my whole desire: that my heart be united to You.

CHAPTER 14

On the Ardent Desire Some Devout People Have for the Body of Christ

DISCIPLE: *How great is Your goodness, O Lord, which You have stored up for those who fear You* (Ps 31:20). When I think of some devout people who approach the Blessed Sacrament with such reverence and devotion, often I am ashamed of myself that I come to Your altar so cold and wanting in affection.

I am not on fire in Your presence, nor do I feel so drawn to You as do many devout souls, who desire so intensely to receive You in Communion that the emotion of their heart causes them to weep, and from the depths of their soul they eagerly long for You, my God, the living fountain. There is no other way their hunger can be satisfied except by receiving Your Body with joy and spiritual eagerness.

2. The ardent faith of these people is certainly a living proof of Your sacred presence! Truly they know their Lord in the breaking of bread; for their hearts burn strongly within them when Jesus walks with them. Such impulse and devotion, such ardent love and strong fervor are too often wanting in me.

O good Jesus, so kind and gracious, be merciful to me, Your poorest servant; grant that at least sometimes I may feel a spark of Your love stirring my heart when I receive You in Holy Communion, for the strengthening of my faith, the increase of my hope; and that charity, once enkindled by tasting the heavenly manna, will never fail.

3. This grace I so desire You will give me, in Your mercy, at the time Your will deems best; then You will visit me with the spirit of fervor.

Even though I do not burn with such fervor as those special souls so completely devoted to You, yet I long to have this same fervor, hoping and praying that I may be one of those fervent lovers of Yours and be numbered in their holy company.

CHAPTER 15

That the Grace of Devotion Is Obtained by Humility and Self-Denial

CHRIST: You must seek the grace of devotion with perseverance, waiting for it with patience and confidence, gratefully receiving it, humbly keeping it and carefully using it. The time and manner of this heavenly visit you must leave to God—until He wills to come to you.

You should especially humble yourself when you feel little or no devotion; but do not be downcast or too upset about this. Often God is pleased to give in a single moment what He has withheld for a long time, sometimes bestowing at the end of prayer what He delayed giving when first you began to pray for it.

2. If grace always was given at once and was ever present for the asking, the weak person would be unable to bear it. Therefore, wait for the grace of devotion with good hope and humble patience. However, you must blame yourself and your sins when it is either not given or secretly taken away.

Sometimes it is something very trivial that prevents or hides grace—if it is proper to call trifling so great and important a good. But if you remove and perfectly overcome this obstacle, large or small, then your desire will be granted to you.

3. When you have wholeheartedly delivered yourself up to God, seeking neither this thing nor that, according to your own wish or will, but placing yourself entirely in His care, you will find yourself united to Him in peace; for nothing will so satisfy you or give you greater pleasure than the will of God being accomplished in you.

Therefore, raise up your intention to God in all simplicity, detaching yourself from all disordered love or dislike of any creature; then you will be more apt to receive grace and more worthy to be given the gift of devotion. Where the Lord finds vessels empty, He fills them with His blessings.

The more perfectly persons abandon worldly things and the more they rid themselves of self-love through contempt of self, the sooner grace will come, the more abundantly it will enter in, and the higher it will lift their liberated hearts.

4. Then shall they see and be enriched and their hearts shall wonder and be enlarged within them, for the hand of our Lord is with them forever. See how blessed are those who seek God with their whole heart and who do not presume on their soul's salvation! When they receive the Blessed Sacrament, such persons obtain the grace of union with God, because they do not seek their own devotion and consolation but the honor and glory of God above all.

CHAPTER 16

That We Should Reveal Our Needs to Christ and Ask His Grace

DISCIPLE: O most sweet and loving Lord, Whom I now desire to receive devoutly, You know my weakness and my needs. You know the great evils and sinful tendencies that weigh me down; how I am dispirited, tempted, grieved and defiled.

I come to You for remedy and I pray to You for consolation and relief. You Who know all things—even my inmost self—and Who alone can perfectly comfort and help me, it is to You I make my plea. You know what I need the most and that I am weak in the practice of virtue.

2. See me standing before You, destitute and naked, begging for Your grace and imploring Your mercy. Give food to this hungry beggar, inflame my heart with the fire of Your love and enlighten my blindness with the light of Your presence. Turn all earthly things into bitterness for me, all things that burden and annoy me into patience, and make me despise and forget all worldly things.

Let me lift up my heart to You in heaven and do not permit me to roam the face of the earth. May You alone be my delight—now and forever. Only You are my food and drink, my love and my joy, my sweetness and all my good.

3. Oh, if only You would set me on fire, completely consume me and transform me into Your-

self, so that I may become one with You by the grace of inward union, and by the melting power of ardent love! Do not let this hungry and dry soul depart from You; but, in Your kindness, deal with me mercifully, as You so wonderfully dealt with Your Saints.

How marvelous it would be if I were to be completely inflamed by You and die to myself; for You are the eternally burning and never-failing fire, a love which purifies the heart and enlightens the understanding!

CHAPTER 17

On a Burning Love and Eager Desire to Receive Christ

D*ISCIPLE:* With all devotion and ardent love, with all the affectionate longing of my heart, my Lord and my God, I desire to receive You, just as many Saints and devout souls, whose holiness of life and burning devotion were especially pleasing to You, have desired to receive You in Holy Communion.

Blessed Lord, eternal love, my highest good and never-ending joy, I desire to receive You with such longing and reverence as any of the Saints have had, or ever could have experienced.

2. Of course, I am unworthy to have all those feelings of devotion; nevertheless I offer You the entire love of my heart, just as if I were the only one with those most pleasing and burning desires. Whatever a devout mind can think of or long for I offer to You, with all due reverence and interior

fervor. I wish to hold nothing back for myself, but, with great freedom and a willing heart, I wish to offer to You my whole being and all that is mine.

O Lord God, my Creator and Redeemer, I desire today to receive You with great affection, reverence, praise and honor, with such gratitude, worthiness and love, and with that faith, hope and purity with which Your holy Mother, the glorious Virgin Mary, desired and received You when she humbly and devoutly answered the Angel Gabriel—who announced the joyous tidings of the mystery of the Incarnation to her—saying: *"I am the servant of the Lord. Let it be done to me according to your word"* (Lk 1:38).

3. Your blessed forerunner—most excellent among the Saints—John the Baptist, in Your presence leaped for joy, through the Holy Spirit, while still in his mother's womb. Later on, when he saw You walking among the people, with utter humility and devout affection he said: *"It is . . . the friend of the bridegroom who stands by and listens to Him and rejoices greatly when he hears the bridegroom's voice"* (Jn 3:29). So I also wish to be inflamed with great and holy desires, and to offer myself to You with all my heart.

For this reason I offer and present to You all the praise of devout hearts, their ardent affections, their ecstasies, their spiritual insights, their heavenly visions, with all the virtues and praises that ever will be offered by all creatures in heaven or on earth. I offer them for myself and for all those for whom I have been asked to pray, that

You may be worthily praised and glorified forever by all human beings.

4. Accept my prayers, O Lord my God, and my desire to give You infinite praise and blessing, which are rightfully due to You because of Your surpassing greatness. All these I give You and desire to give You every day and every moment of time.

With these dispositions and prayers, I invite and entreat all the heavenly spirits, as well as all the faithful, to join with me in thanking and praising You.

5. May all peoples, tribes and tongues praise You, magnifying Your holy and sweet Name with great joy and ardent devotion. May all who, with reverence and devotion, celebrate this most sublime Sacrament and receive it with unwavering faith, deserve to find grace and mercy from You; and may they make supplication for me, a sinner.

When they have obtained the devotion they desired, and that spiritual union with You at Your holy and heavenly altar—being greatly refreshed and consoled—may they remember me, a poor creature.

CHAPTER 18

That People Must Not Curiously Search into This Sacrament, But Be Humble Followers of Christ, Always Submitting Their Senses to Holy Faith

CHRIST: Beware of curious and useless searching into this profound Sacrament, if you do not wish to sink into the depths of doubt. *He who is a searcher of majesty shall he overwhelmed by glory* (Prov 25:27, Vulgate). God's powers are greater than humans can comprehend. You may seek after truth, provided you do so in a humble and docile way—always ready to be taught and to walk in the paths of sound doctrine declared by the Fathers.

2. That simplicity is truly blessed which departs from ways of dispute and follows the plain and sure path of God's commandments. Many have lost their devotion while searching into mysteries too deep for them to understand. Only faith and a good life are required of you, not a lofty intellect nor a probing into the deep mysteries of God.

If you cannot understand or grasp those things which are beneath you, how can you comprehend those that are above you? Submit yourself humbly to God, and submit your senses to faith, and the light of knowledge will be given to you for your spiritual well-being, according to the measure of God.

3. Many people are seriously tempted concerning faith in the Blessed Sacrament through no fault of their own; but rather this is to be blamed on the devil. Do not worry about it, nor argue with your thoughts, and do not answer doubts suggested by this fiend. Instead, put your faith in the words of God, believe His Saints and Prophets, and the wicked enemy will soon leave you alone.

It often profits the servant of God to endure these things. For the devil does not tempt unbelievers and sinners who are already his; rather he tempts and harasses the faithful and devout.

4. Go forward, therefore, in simple and unwavering faith, and approach this Sacrament with humble reverence. Whatever you are unable to understand, confidently entrust to Almighty God. God never deceives you; but those who trust too much in self are deceived.

God walks with the simple, makes Himself known to the humble, and gives understanding to the poor in spirit. He reveals His meaning to the clean of heart, but He hides His grace from the proud and curious. Human reason is weak and easily deceived; but true faith cannot be deceived.

5. All reason and natural inquiry must follow faith, never precede or question it. For in this most holy and exalted Sacrament, faith and love are uppermost and work in hidden ways.

The eternal and incomprehensible God effects great things in heaven and on earth by His infinite power, impossible for us to discover. If God's words could be understood easily by human reason, they would not be considered wonderful and beyond human expression.

PASSAGES IN THE IMITATION OF CHRIST

Suitable to the different states of life and spiritual necessities of the faithful

For priests

Book 1 Chap. 18, 19, 20, 25
2 " 11, 12
3 " 3, 10, 31, 56
4 " 5, 7, 10, 11, 12, 18

For those who live in seminaries

Book 1 Chap. 17,18,19 20,21,25
3 " 2, 3, 10, 31, 56
4 " 5, 7, 10, 11, 12, 18

For students

Book 1 Chap. 1, 2, 3, 5
3 " 2, 38, 43, 44, 58
4 " 18

For those who are grieved at making little progress in their studies

Book 3 Chap. 29, 30, 41, 47

For persons who aspire to piety

Book 1 Chap. 15, 18, 19, 20, 21, 22, 25
2 " 1, 4, 7, 8, 9, 11, 12
3 " 5, 6, 7, 11, 27, 31, 32, 33, 53, 54, 55, 56

For persons in affliction and humiliation

Book 1 Chap. 12
2 " 11, 12
3 " 12, 15, 16, 17, 18, 19, 20, 21, 29, 30, 35, 41, 47, 48,49, 50, 52, 55, 56

For those who are too sensible of sufferings

Book 1 Chap. 12
2 " 12

For those who labor under temptations

Book 1 Chap. 13
2 " 9
3 " 6, 16, 17, 18, 19, 20, 21, 23, 30, 35, 37, 47, 48, 49, 50, 52, 55

For those who suffer interior trials

Book 2 Chap. 3, 9, 11, 12
3 " 7, 12, 16, 17, 18 19 ,20 ,21, 30, 35, 47, 48, 49, 50, 51, 52, 55, 56

For those who are troubled about the future, their health, their fortune, the success of their undertakings

Book 3 Chap. 39

For persons living in the world, or who are distracted with their employments

Book 3 Chap. 38, 53

For those who are assailed with calumnies or lies

Book 2 Chap. 2
3 " 6, 11, 28, 36, 46

For persons who are beginning their conversion

Book 1Chap. 18, 25
2 " 1
3 " 6, 7, 23, 25, 26, 27, 33, 37, 52, 54, 55

For a retreat

Book 3 Chap. 53 Preparation
1 " 20, 21 Preparation
1 " 22 Miseries of man
1 " 23 Death
1 " 24 Judgment and Hell
3 " 14 Judgment and Hell
3 " 48 Heaven
3 " 59 Conclusion

To obtain interior peace

Book 1 Chap. 6, 11
2 " 3, 6
3 " 7, 23, 25, 38

For dissipated persons

Book 1 Chap. 18, 21, 22, 23,2 4
2 " 10, 12
3 " 14, 27, 33, 45, 53, 55

For hardened sinners

Book 1 Chap. 23, 24
3 " 14, 55

For indolent persons

Book 3 Chap. 24, 27

For those who hear lies

Book 1 Chap. 4

For those who are inclined to pride

Book 1 Chap. 7, 14
2 " 11
3 " 7, 8, 9, 11, 13, 14, 40, 52

For querulous and obstinate persons

Book 1 Chap. 9
3 " 13, 32, 44

For impatient persons

Book 3 Chap. 15, 16, 17, 18, 19
(PAR. 5—Prayer to obtain patience)

For the disobedient

Book 1 Chap. 9
3 " 13, 32

For those who are given to much talking

Book 1 Chap. 10
3 " 24, 44, 45

For those who busy themselves about the faults of others and neglect their own

Book 1 Chap. 11, 14, 16
2 " 5

For those whose devotion is false or badly directed

Book 3 Chap. 4, 6, 7

To direct the intention

Book 3 Chap. 9

For those who are too susceptible

Book 3 Chap. 44

For those who are too much attached to the delights of human friendship

Book 1 Chap. 8, 10
2 " 7, 8
3 " 32, 42, 45

For those who take offense at the simplicity or the obscurity of the Holy Scriptures

Book 1 Chap. 5

For those who are inclined to jealousy

Book 3 Chap. 22, 41

PRAYERS FROM THE IMITATION OF CHRIST

Before spiritual reading

Book 3 Chap. 2

To obtain the grace of devotion

Book 3 Chap. 3 Par. 6 and 7

For the help of divine consolation

Book 3 Chap. 5 Par. 1 and 2
(Before or after Communion)

To obtain an increase of the love of God

Book 3 Chap. 5 Par. 6

Acts of abasement in the presence of God

Book 3 Chap. 8

(Before Communion)

For one who lives in retirement and piety

Book 3 Chap. 10

Acts of profound humility

Book 3 Chap. 14

(Before or after Communion)

For resignation to the will of God

Book 3 Chap. 15, Par. 1, verses 2, 3, and 4
Par. 2, verse 3 to the end

Acts of resignation

Book 3 Chap 16 to the end
Ibid. " 17 Par. 2 and 4
Ibid. " 18 Par. 2

For patience

Book 3 Chap. 19 Par. 5

For one in affliction or temptation

Book 3 Chap. 20, 21, Par 1, 2, 3, 4, 5

(This same prayer for those who experience the eye of God)

(Before or after Communion)

An act of thanksgiving

Book 3 Chap. 21, Par. 7

(After Communion)

For those who think they have received less from God than others, either for body or for soul

Book 3 Chap. 22

For purity of mind and detachment from creatures

Book 3 Chap. 23, Par. 5 to the end

For one who is beginning his conversion

Book 3 Chap. 26

(The same for one who is desirous of advancing in virtue)

To obtain the spirit of strength and wisdom

Book 3 Chap. 27, Par. 4 and 5

For a person in great affliction

Book 3 Chap. 29

Prayer after Communion

Book 3 Chap. 34

(The same to excite one's self to the love of God)

Acts of resignation and reliance on Divine Providence

Book 3 Chap. 39, Par. 2

An act of humility

Book 3 Chap. 40

(Before or after Communion)

When we receive any grace from God

Book 3 Chap. 40

An act of resignation

(Before or after Communion)

Book 3 Chap. 41, Par. 2

Pious sentiments

Book 3 Chap. 44, Par. 2

When attacked with calumny

Book 3 Chap. 46, Par. 5

Prayer on the happiness of Heaven

(Which may be said particularly on the Feasts of Easter, the Ascension, and all Saints)

Book 3 Chap. 48

(Before or after Communion)

Acts of humility and contrition

Book 3 Chap. 52

(Before Communion)

To obtain grace

Book 3 Chap. 55

For priests and religious, to obtain perseverance in their vocations

Book 3 Chap. 56, Par. 3, 5, 6

An act of confidence in God

Book 3 Chap. 57, Par. 4

For all Christians who aspire to piety

Book 3 Chap. 59

(After Communion, or at the conclusion of a Retreat)

In presence of the Blessed Sacrament

Book 4 Chap. 1, 2, 3, 4, 9,11 (to par. 6), 13, 14, 16 17, and part of the prayers above

The dignity of priests, and the sanctity of their ministry

Book 4 Chap. 5

For priests and those in seminaries

Book 4 Chap. 11, Par. 6, 7, and 8